How to Complain to Your Bank: A Clear and Simple Guide to Bank Complaint Resolution

How to Complain, Volume 2

Rebecca Bailey

Published by Trustwell Books, 2025.

HOW TO COMPLAIN TO YOUR BANK: A CLEAR AND SIMPLE GUIDE TO BANK COMPLAINT RESOLUTION

First edition. November 23, 2025.

ISBN: 979-8232685690

Written by Rebecca Bailey.

Table of Contents

Dedication

For everyone who has felt ignored, dismissed, or spoken over by their bank.

You deserve fairness, clarity, and respect.

This book is for you, so your voice is heard and your rights are protected.

"Fairness is not given. You claim it by speaking clearly, standing firm, and refusing to be ignored."

Introduction

Banks hold an important place in daily life. People use them for wages, bills, savings, borrowing, and payments. Because banks control access to money, any problem becomes stressful very quickly. When payments fail, transfers are delayed, cards stop working, or decisions are made without clear reasons, the impact can be immediate. Many people try to fix issues by calling customer services or visiting their local branch, only to find that the explanations they receive are unclear or incomplete. This is why understanding the complaints process matters. When you know your rights and understand how banks should respond, you stay in control even when the situation is difficult.

A bank complaint is not a request for help. It is a formal process that triggers clear duties under the Financial Conduct Authority rules. These rules require banks to investigate concerns properly, provide clear outcomes, and treat customers fairly. The rules apply to every bank in the United Kingdom. They apply to traditional high street banks, digital only banks, building societies, credit card issuers, and financial service firms that handle money. When you make a complaint, you activate rights that protect you. This book explains those rights in a clear and simple way.

Many people feel unsure about raising complaints with their bank. Some feel that the bank will ignore them. Others believe the process is complicated. Some worry that complaining will make things worse. In reality, the opposite is true. A clear complaint ensures that the bank treats your case seriously. Banks must follow strict rules when handling complaints. They must respond within set timeframes. They must look at all the evidence. They must explain their decision. They cannot close the case without giving you a final answer. These rules exist to protect consumers and ensure fairness.

This book guides you through the full complaints process. Banks work differently from councils or housing associations. They do not use a multi stage complaint model. They follow a single formal complaints process that leads to a final response. Once that final response is issued, you can go to the Financial Ombudsman Service. Because banks use a single stage system, the quality of your initial complaint matters even more. You have one opportunity to explain what went wrong, provide evidence, and show the impact. This book explains how to do that with clarity and confidence.

Understanding why complaints fail will help you avoid common mistakes. Many complaints fail because they focus only on the outcome rather than the reasons behind the issue. For example, a customer might simply say that a payment was delayed, but they do not describe the impact or provide evidence. A customer might say that a charge is unfair but they do not explain why. Banks rely heavily on internal records. When information is missing, unclear, or incomplete, banks fall back on their assumptions. This often leads to decisions that do not reflect the full truth of the situation. A strong complaint removes uncertainty and makes it easier for the bank to investigate properly.

Another common problem is that customers accept explanations that do not address all points. Banks sometimes provide long responses that appear detailed but avoid the main issue. Once you finish this book, you will know how to recognise responses that are incomplete or unclear. You will know how to challenge gaps in the investigation. You will understand what a fair response looks like, what evidence banks should review, and how they should explain their reasoning. This knowledge increases your confidence and helps you judge the fairness of the process.

The Financial Ombudsman Service plays an important role in the complaints journey. Banks know that poor investigations can be overturned by the Ombudsman. This is why understanding the Ombudsman process is useful even before you reach that stage. The Ombudsman looks at evidence, communication, policy, and fairness. They focus on what is reasonable, what is accurate, and what should have been done. They do not rely on bank policy alone. They look at the wider picture. This book explains when to escalate to the Ombudsman, how to prepare your case, and what information matters most.

Legislation and regulation also shape the complaints process. The Financial Services and Markets Act provides the legal foundation for financial regulation in the United Kingdom. The Financial Conduct Authority rules guide how banks must treat customers. The dispute resolution rules set out how complaints must be handled, how quickly banks must respond, and what they must include in their final response. These rules protect you, and this book explains the parts you need in simple language. You do not need specialist knowledge. You only need a clear understanding of how the system works.

A strong complaint is not about sounding angry or using complex language. A strong complaint is structured, factual, and organised. It describes what happened, when it happened, and why it was wrong. It includes evidence. It explains the impact. It states what you want to happen next. When you follow this structure, you give the bank the information it needs to investigate the issue properly. You also make it easier for the Ombudsman to understand your case if escalation becomes necessary.

Many people do not know that banks must keep you updated during their investigation. They must tell you if they need more time. They must give you a final response within eight weeks. If they do not, you can escalate your complaint even without a final response. These rules exist to prevent banks from delaying cases or leaving customers without answers. Knowing your rights ensures that you can challenge unfair delays and protect yourself from long periods of uncertainty.

This book is written for anyone who has struggled to get clear answers from their bank. It is for people who have been told conflicting information. It is for people who have lost money due to errors. It is for people who feel that the bank is not listening. When you understand the complaints process, you do not feel powerless. You know what to expect. You know how to prepare. You know how to challenge responses that are incomplete or unfair. This book gives you that confidence.

The aim of this book is not to make the process more complicated. It is to make it easier. When you see the complaints process for what it is, you see that it follows clear steps. You explain the issue. The bank investigates. They provide an outcome. You assess the fairness of the outcome. If the outcome is not fair, you escalate. The process is simple when explained clearly. The challenge comes from poor communication and weak investigations. This book helps you recognise those issues and respond effectively.

By the end of this book, you will understand every stage of the complaints process. You will know your rights. You will know how banks investigate concerns. You will know how to write clear and effective complaints. You will know how to challenge unfair decisions. You will know how to escalate to the Ombudsman. You will understand what decisions mean and what remedies are available. Most importantly, you will know how to stay in control from the start of the complaint to the end.

Chapter 1
Understanding How Banks Operate

Banks operate through a mixture of automated systems, risk controls, internal processes, and regulated duties. When you raise a complaint, the bank does not begin from a blank page. They begin from the information stored in their systems. This information includes transaction logs, account notes, risk alerts, communication records, and previous decisions. Understanding how these systems work helps you see why problems occur and how to challenge them properly.

Banks rely heavily on automated systems to run day to day operations. When you make a payment, check your balance, transfer money, or use your card, a large part of the process takes place without human involvement. Automated rules check for unusual behaviour, verify payment details, and decide whether a transaction is approved. These rules are controlled by algorithms that follow strict patterns. When something falls outside the expected pattern, the system reacts. This reaction can include blocking a payment, flagging an alert, or putting a temporary hold on your account. These actions happen before a human adviser ever sees the case.

Advisers rely on information from these systems when speaking to you. When you call your bank, the adviser reads from internal screens that show limited pieces of information. Some screens display your account balance. Others show pending transactions. Others show alerts or notes. Advisers do not see everything at once. They navigate between different screens, often while trying to keep up with your explanation. This increases the chance that they misunderstand the issue or overlook something important. This is not deliberate. It is a limitation of the systems they use. When you understand this, you can explain your issue in a clear structure that helps the adviser find the right information.

Internal notes form another important part of bank operations. When you contact your bank, the adviser is required to record a note of the call. These notes guide future decisions. If a note is incomplete or inaccurate, other staff may repeat the error. Notes may be written quickly, and some advisers record only a summary of the discussion. Important details may be missing. When a complaint is raised, the complaint handler will read these notes. If the notes are unclear, the complaint handler may make incorrect assumptions. This is why clear and structured complaints are essential. They help correct the record and prevent the bank from relying solely on incomplete notes.

Banks also divide responsibilities between different teams. Customer service teams handle general enquiries. Fraud teams handle suspicious activity. Dispute teams handle chargebacks and transaction investigations. Specialist teams handle specific services such as mortgages or loans. Complaint teams are separate and have access to more information, but even they may need to request details from other teams. When your case moves between teams, you may receive different explanations, especially if one team has access to information that another does not. Understanding this helps you identify when the bank's explanation may be missing important evidence.

Banks also follow internal policies. These policies guide staff decisions. Policies cover matters such as fraud checks, service standards, customer contact rules, payment investigations, and risk controls. Policies differ between banks, but all banks must follow the rules set by the Financial Conduct Authority. Policies cannot override regulation. When you complain, some staff may rely on internal policy because they believe it is correct. This can lead to incorrect decisions. When you know the regulatory framework, you can challenge decisions that rely solely on internal policy instead of the proper rules.

Transaction records form a core part of bank operations. Banks keep detailed logs of payments, including timestamps, locations, authorisation methods, and device information. These logs help banks understand how payments were made. Staff may not always check these logs unless you raise a dispute. Some advisers may rely on the balance or transaction list, which shows only part of the information. When you dispute a payment, it is important that the bank reviews the full logs. If they do not, the investigation may be incomplete. Clear complaints help direct the bank to the correct evidence.

Fraud systems operate independently of customer service. These systems use automated checks to identify unusual behaviour. If something appears unusual, the system may block transactions or restrict access. Fraud teams then review the alerts. Fraud teams often have limited contact with customers. They follow strict procedures and may not explain the details of their checks. When a fraud block occurs, you may receive generic explanations. These explanations can feel unclear because staff cannot reveal all internal processes. Understanding that fraud checks are automated helps you challenge unclear reasoning.

Banks also keep call recordings. Not every call is recorded, but many are. Complaint handlers can request call recordings to verify what happened. However, call recordings may be stored in separate systems. Retrieving them takes time. Some banks retrieve only key recordings. If you refer specifically to a call in your complaint, you increase the chance that the bank will listen to it. Clear references to dates, times, and what was said help the complaint handler locate the correct recording. When you do not provide these details, the bank may rely on incomplete notes instead.

Online banking records form another important part of the bank's evidence. They monitor login attempts, device information, account changes, and communication through secure messages. When you raise a complaint about online banking, the bank must review these logs. Some complaint responses fail because the bank does not review electronic records properly. When you understand what information exists, you can request that the bank reviews specific logs. This helps strengthen your case.

Another area where problems occur is payment processing. Payments pass through several steps before reaching the recipient. The bank checks the details, the system processes the request, and the payment moves through internal and external networks. Delays can occur at any stage. Some delays occur before the bank sends the payment. Others occur after the payment leaves the bank. When delays happen, staff may struggle to identify the cause unless they check the full payment path. If they do not, you may receive vague explanations. When you complain, a clear timeline helps the bank trace the delay.

Direct debits follow a different process. They are controlled by the Direct Debit Guarantee, which requires immediate refunds when payments are taken incorrectly. Some advisers may not understand the guarantee fully and may direct you to contact the merchant. This is incorrect. When you know the rules, you can ask the bank to follow the proper process. Understanding how direct debits work helps you challenge incorrect advice.

Standing orders operate differently again. They are controlled by the bank, not the merchant. When a standing order fails, the cause is usually within the bank's control. Complaints about standing orders often relate to incorrect setup or internal errors. Understanding the difference between direct debits and standing orders helps you identify the correct complaint route.

Banks also follow service level agreements for internal tasks. These agreements set expectations for how quickly tasks should be completed. They may cover updating information, reviewing alerts, processing payments, or responding to enquiries. When internal delays occur, they may not be visible to advisers. This can lead to inconsistent explanations. Clear complaints help ensure the bank reviews internal delays as part of the investigation.

Understanding how banks manage customer data is also important. Banks store personal information, transaction details, and communication history. When errors appear in your data, they can affect decisions. Some errors arise from outdated information. Others arise from incorrect entries. When you complain, it is important to point out any errors clearly. This helps ensure the bank updates your information and reviews decisions made using incorrect data.

Banks also use internal scoring systems. These systems assess risk, credit behaviour, and account activity. Scoring systems influence decisions such as card limits, account restrictions, or service eligibility. Staff may not always understand how these scores are generated. Scores are often produced automatically and updated regularly. When you complain about decisions influenced by scoring, you may need to direct the bank to review the underlying data.

Understanding these operational details helps you recognise where mistakes happen. Banks rely on systems, policies, and automated rules. Human advisers interpret information from these systems. When information is missing or incorrect, problems occur. A strong complaint provides clear facts and directs the bank to the correct evidence. This increases the chance of a fair outcome and reduces the risk of repeated errors.

Banks must also follow strict rules when handling customer money. These rules come from the Financial Conduct Authority. The rules require banks to keep customer funds safe, protect against fraud, treat customers fairly, and communicate clearly. These duties affect how staff respond to enquiries and how complaints are handled. When a bank fails to follow these rules, the impact can be serious. Understanding the regulatory framework helps you identify when something has gone wrong and how to raise it in your complaint.

Another important part of bank operations is how they handle errors. Errors can occur at many points. A branch adviser may enter information incorrectly. A system may apply a rule to the wrong account. A payment may fail due to incorrect data. A fraud alert may be triggered incorrectly. When errors occur, the bank should correct them promptly. However, errors are not always identified quickly. Staff may not recognise that an issue is caused by an error. This can lead to explanations that do not reflect the true cause. When you describe your issue clearly, you help the bank identify errors more quickly and correct them.

Many bank decisions are based on rules rather than personal judgement. When you apply for a product such as an overdraft or loan, the bank runs automated checks. These checks consider your credit history, account usage, income patterns, and risk score. Staff may not be able to explain the full details of these checks. They may give general explanations that do not match your situation. When you complain about decisions like these, you can ask the bank to explain what information was used. This helps you understand whether the decision was fair and whether any errors influenced the outcome.

Banks also use internal escalation processes when they need more time or specialist help. If an adviser cannot resolve the issue, they may pass the case to another team. This may cause delays, especially if the case moves between several teams. Understanding the internal structure helps you challenge delays. When you know which teams are involved, you can ask specific questions. This reduces the chance of the bank giving vague explanations and helps them identify where the delay occurred.

Communication between teams is not always smooth. One team may not update records correctly. Another team may not receive all the information they need. This can lead to repeated questions or contradictory explanations. When advisers rely on incomplete information, they may respond incorrectly. When you raise a complaint, the complaint handler must bring together information from all teams. This is why clear, structured complaints are important. They help the complaint handler identify gaps and request the correct information.

Another key part of bank operations is how they handle disputed transactions. When you dispute a card payment, the bank must follow card scheme rules. These rules apply to all UK banks and require the bank to raise a chargeback when certain conditions are met. Staff must review the transaction details carefully. They may need to check whether the payment used chip and PIN, contactless, online authentication, or card details only. Some staff do not understand these differences fully. When you know which evidence the bank must check, you can ask them to review the correct information.

Disputed direct debits follow a different process. The Direct Debit Guarantee gives you the right to an immediate refund if a payment is taken incorrectly. Some advisers may not understand the guarantee properly and may direct you to contact the merchant. This is not correct. The bank must issue the refund and investigate afterwards. When you complain, you can refer to the guarantee to ensure the bank follows the correct process.

Banks also handle standing orders differently. Standing orders are controlled by the bank, not the merchant. When a standing order fails, the bank must investigate the cause internally. This may involve checking system logs, scheduled payment rules, or manual errors. Understanding the difference between these payment types helps you challenge incorrect explanations and direct the bank to the correct evidence.

Banks use a layered security model to protect accounts. This includes monitoring login attempts, checking device information, and reviewing network activity. When unusual activity is detected, the bank may restrict account access. These restrictions can cause stress and disruption. Staff may not explain the reason clearly because they cannot reveal security rules. When you complain about account restrictions, it is important to provide a clear timeline of events and explain the impact. This helps the bank review the case properly and remove restrictions if they were applied incorrectly.

Many customers do not realise that banks keep detailed records of online banking activity. These records include login times, device details, IP addresses, and security events. When something goes wrong, these records help the bank understand what happened. If the bank does not review these records as part of a complaint, the investigation may be incomplete. When you know what information exists, you can ask the bank to review specific records. This helps ensure the investigation is thorough.

Another important area is communication. Banks send letters, emails, and secure messages. These messages use templates that may not address your specific issue. Templates are used to save time but can result in generic explanations. When a response feels generic, it may indicate that the bank has not reviewed your case properly. When you complain, you can point out when the explanation does not address your specific situation. This encourages the bank to provide a clearer and more accurate response.

Banks also use internal deadlines for tasks such as processing payments, responding to enquiries, or reviewing alerts. When these deadlines are missed, delays occur. Staff may not always understand why a delay happened. They may give general explanations. When you provide a timeline in your complaint, you help the bank identify delays and correct them. Timelines also help the Ombudsman understand the issue clearly if escalation becomes necessary.

Understanding how banks store and access evidence also helps you prepare a stronger complaint. Banks keep communication records, payment logs, fraud alerts, internal notes, and system changes. When you know which evidence matters, you can ask the bank to review the correct records. This strengthens your complaint and increases the chance of a fair outcome.

Banks also rely on commercial arrangements with card networks and payment providers. These arrangements influence how disputes are handled and how long investigations take. Banks must follow the rules set by these networks. When you understand the rules, you can challenge delays or incorrect decisions. This ensures the bank follows the proper process.

Knowing how banks operate gives you the foundation needed to approach the complaints process with confidence. You understand where errors occur, why staff give conflicting information, and how internal systems influence decisions. You also understand the limits of what staff can see and how complaints teams gather information. This knowledge helps you prepare clear and effective complaints that guide the bank toward the correct evidence.

Chapter 2
Your Rights When Dealing with a Bank

Banks must follow strict rules when dealing with customers. These rules protect you when something goes wrong. When you understand your rights, you can challenge poor decisions, recognise unfair treatment, and insist on proper investigations. Banks must follow the Financial Conduct Authority rules. These rules apply to every bank in the United Kingdom. They apply to high street banks, digital banks, building societies, credit card providers, and financial service firms that handle money. The rules set out how banks must treat you, how they must communicate, and how they must investigate complaints. Understanding these rights helps you stay in control of the process from the start.

The Financial Conduct Authority sets standards for how banks must behave. These standards are known as the Principles for Businesses. They are simple, clear statements that banks must follow at all times. One principle requires banks to treat customers fairly. Another requires clear communication. Another requires proper systems and controls. When a bank fails to follow these principles, the service may become unfair. When you complain, these principles guide how the bank should review your case. Understanding the principles helps you identify when something has gone wrong and how to explain it in your complaint.

Your rights are also shaped by detailed rules called the dispute resolution rules. These rules tell banks how to handle complaints. The rules require banks to acknowledge complaints quickly, investigate them properly, and issue a final response within eight weeks. These rules protect customers from delays. If a bank fails to issue a final response within eight weeks, you have the right to escalate your complaint to the Financial Ombudsman Service. This prevents cases from being left unresolved for long periods. When you understand the eight-week rule, you can insist on progress and avoid unnecessary delays.

Banks must also provide clear communication. This is another key right. When responding to complaints, banks must explain their decisions. They must say whether they uphold or reject the complaint. They must give reasons.. They must refer to the evidence they reviewed. When a response does not do this, it may not meet the required standards. Understanding this helps you recognise when a bank's investigation is incomplete. If the explanation is vague, generic, or does not address your main points, you can challenge it directly. Clear communication is not optional. It is a requirement.

Another important right is the right to fair treatment. The Financial Conduct Authority's rules require banks to consider your individual circumstances. They must look at the facts of your case. They must recognise vulnerabilities, financial pressure, and any distress caused by errors. They must not apply rules in a rigid or unfair way. When a decision feels harsh or does not consider your circumstances, you can challenge it based on your right to fair treatment. When you describe your circumstances clearly in your complaint, you help the bank meet this duty.

Banks must also investigate complaints thoroughly. This is another important right. A thorough investigation means the bank must check all relevant evidence. They must review transaction logs, call recordings, online activity, notes, policy documents, and internal records. They cannot rely on assumptions. They cannot ignore evidence that is available. They cannot close a complaint without checking important information. When you know what evidence exists, you can ask the bank to review specific records. This helps ensure the investigation is complete.

Another essential right is the right to a proper final response. A final response must explain the outcome clearly. It must say whether the bank upholds the complaint fully, partially, or not at all. It must explain how the decision was reached. It must include information about your right to go to the Financial Ombudsman Service. If the response does not include this information, it may not be valid. When you know what a final response must contain, you can judge whether the bank has followed the correct process.

You also have the right to redress when the bank has made an error. Redress may include refunds, corrections to records, interest payments, or compensation for distress. Banks must offer fair redress based on the impact of the error. When you describe the impact clearly in your complaint, you help the bank understand what redress is appropriate. Impact is not about emotion. It is about the practical effect of the error. When your wages are delayed, you may miss payments. When a fraud block is incorrect, you may be left without access to money. When a card fails, you may be unable to complete important purchases. These effects help the bank understand the seriousness of the issue.

Banks must also protect your personal data. When data is incorrect, incomplete, or misused, you may have the right to request corrections or raise concerns. Incorrect data can lead to incorrect decisions. When you identify errors in your bank data, you can ask the bank to correct them. This is an important right that helps prevent future problems. Clear complaints help ensure that records are corrected properly.

Another important right is the right to access information. Banks must provide copies of certain information when requested. This may include transaction logs, notes, or communication records. Some information may require a subject access request, which is governed by data protection law. When you understand what information you can request, you can gather the evidence needed to support your complaint. This helps you challenge decisions that rely on incorrect or incomplete information.

The Financial Ombudsman Service plays a major role in protecting your rights. The Ombudsman is independent and must make fair decisions based on the facts. When a bank fails to follow the rules, the Ombudsman can order the bank to put things right. This may include refunds, corrections, or compensation. You have the right to go to the Ombudsman once you receive a final response or once eight weeks have passed. Understanding this right gives you confidence in the process. You are not limited to the bank's view. An independent body will review the case if needed.

Banks must also identify and support vulnerable customers. This is another right that many people do not know about. Vulnerability can arise from health problems, financial difficulties, bereavement, caring responsibilities, language barriers, or other challenges. When a customer is vulnerable, banks must take extra care. They must communicate clearly. They must avoid unreasonable demands. They must ensure that the customer understands the information. When you explain your circumstances in your complaint, you help the bank meet its duties.

Another important right is the right to challenge decisions. If a bank rejects your complaint or provides an explanation that does not address your concerns, you have the right to respond and ask for a review. Banks must consider your points. They cannot refuse to review a complaint without giving proper reasons. When you understand this right, you can insist on a proper review when needed.

You also have the right to clarity when disputes involve third parties. For example, when payments involve merchants, card issuers, or payment networks, the bank must explain who is responsible for what. They must not direct you away without explaining why. When you know how responsibilities are shared, you can challenge incorrect explanations and ensure the bank handles your complaint correctly.

Your rights also include protection from unfair outcomes. When the bank's decision does not match the evidence, you can challenge it. When the bank fails to consider important information, you can raise this in your complaint. When the bank relies on incorrect assumptions, you can correct them with clear facts. The Ombudsman can review the case if the bank does not resolve it properly.

Banks must also provide fair access to accounts and services. When accounts are restricted or services are withdrawn, the bank must explain why in clear terms. Some restrictions are required by law, but others come from internal policies. When you understand the difference, you can challenge incorrect restrictions.

Another important right is the right to a clear explanation of charges and fees. Banks must explain why charges were applied. They must ensure charges are fair and transparent. When a charge is incorrect or unclear, you can challenge it through the complaints process.

These rights give you the foundation needed to approach complaints with confidence. When you understand the rules, you can ensure the bank follows them. When you describe your issue clearly, the bank must investigate it properly. When you recognise unfair outcomes, you can challenge them. When you understand your right to escalate, you know how to take the complaint forward if needed.

Your rights also include the right to accurate information. Banks must ensure the information they give you is correct. When you ask about a payment, a balance, a fee, or a process, the explanation must be clear and factual. Advisers must not guess. They must not give incomplete answers. They must not avoid questions. When you receive information that does not appear correct, you have the right to challenge it. You can ask the bank to check the information again. You can ask them to review the records. You can ask for a clear explanation in writing. This helps you avoid reliance on verbal statements that may be contradictory or unclear.

You also have the right to raise concerns about poor service. Poor service includes delays, errors, incorrect advice, lack of updates, lost documents, repeated mistakes, and unhelpful communication. Poor service also includes situations where the bank fails to explain decisions or fails to respond within a reasonable time. When you raise a complaint about service, the bank must investigate the issue. They must consider the impact. They must address the failures. They must explain what they will do to prevent it happening again. The right to complain about service standards is important, as it helps improve the way banks operate.

Your rights also include protection from financial harm. When the bank makes a mistake that causes you to lose money, they must put things right. This can include reversing charges, refunding payments, restoring balances, correcting interest, or fixing records that led to financial loss. When you explain the impact clearly, the bank must consider this. Financial harm does not need to be extreme. It can include missed bills, overdraft charges, or late payment markers. These are important points for the bank to consider when deciding redress.

Banks must also follow rules that protect customers during financial difficulty. If you are struggling with money, the bank must treat you with extra care. They must avoid taking actions that increase pressure. They must offer support where possible. They must communicate in a way that is easy to understand. When a bank fails to do this, it may be a breach of regulatory expectations. When you explain your circumstances in your complaint, you help the bank recognise their duties.

Another key right is the right to be kept informed during the complaints process. Banks must update you at key points. They must acknowledge the complaint. They must tell you if they need more time. They must explain why more time is needed. They must provide a final response within eight weeks. When updates are missing or unclear, you can challenge this. Lack of updates can indicate that the bank has not investigated the complaint properly.

You also have the right to bring new information at any time. If you receive new evidence or realise something was missed, you can send the information to the bank. They must consider it if it is relevant. They cannot refuse to look at new evidence without good reason. This protects you from situations where important details appear later.

Your rights also give you the ability to request that the bank checks specific records. If a payment failed, you can ask them to review the payment logs. If you were given incorrect advice, you can ask them to check the call recording. If your card was blocked, you can ask them to review the security events. If an adviser said something different from the written response, you can ask them to check the notes. This ensures the investigation is based on facts rather than assumptions.

Banks must also handle complaints in a way that is not biased. This is a core right. Banks cannot allow internal targets, financial pressures, or personal views to influence complaints. They must consider the facts. They must follow the evidence. They must follow the rules. When you recognise signs of bias, you can raise this in your complaint. Examples include dismissing evidence without explanation, ignoring clear information, or relying only on internal policy when regulation contradicts it.

You also have the right to clarity about who is responsible for resolving the issue. Some issues involve more than one organisation. For example, card transactions involve the merchant, the card scheme, and the bank. International payments involve several banks. Disputes involving card providers may involve third parties. When responsibility is split, the bank must explain who is responsible for what. They must not direct you away without a clear reason. They must explain the role of each organisation. This helps you understand the correct route to resolution.

Another important right is protection from unfair treatment when errors occur. Everyone makes mistakes, including banks. When the bank makes an error, they must correct it. They must not blame the customer for the bank's mistake. They must not ignore evidence that shows the error. They must not close a complaint without addressing the issue. When you understand this right, you can challenge attempts to dismiss errors.

You also have the right to a clear explanation of how decisions were reached. A bank cannot simply state the outcome. They must explain the reasoning. They must show how they used the evidence. They must explain which records were checked. They must explain why they reached their conclusion. When explanations are unclear, incomplete, or contradictory, you can challenge them directly.

Banks must also ensure their staff are competent. Staff must understand the processes they use. They must give correct information. They must follow the rules. When staff provide incorrect advice, this can lead to poor outcomes. When you complain, the bank must review the advice given and correct any errors. This protects you from decisions that were made on the basis of incorrect information.

You also have the right to complain without fear of negative consequences. Banks must not penalise customers for raising complaints. They cannot close accounts or restrict services because you complained. They cannot treat you differently. Complaints are a protected process. This right encourages customers to raise concerns without fear.

Your rights also include protection when the bank makes decisions based on automated systems. Automated decisions must be fair. They must be based on correct data. When automated decisions cause problems, you can challenge them. You can ask the bank to review the decision manually. They must do so when the automated process appears incorrect or unfair.

Another important right is the right to escalate your complaint. Once the bank issues a final response, or once eight weeks pass without a final response, you can take your case to the Financial Ombudsman Service. This right ensures that banks cannot be the final judge of their own decisions. A fully independent body will review the case. The Ombudsman has the power to overturn unfair decisions and order redress.

You also have the right to clarity about compensation. When the bank offers compensation, they must explain what it covers. They must ensure it reflects the impact of the issue. They must follow fair guidelines. Compensation is not a favour. It is a form of redress when service has been poor. When compensation is too low, you can challenge it based on the impact you described.

Banks must also provide information that helps customers understand their accounts. This includes statements, transaction records, interest details, and fee information. When information is missing or unclear, you can request clarification. Banks must respond. When they fail to provide clear information, it may affect the fairness of decisions. When you complain, you can ask them to explain any unclear entries or charges.

Your rights also include the right to a transparent investigation. Banks must consider the evidence you provide. They must not dismiss information without explanation. They must explain when evidence cannot be obtained and why. This prevents investigations from being rushed or incomplete.

Finally, you have the right to resolution. Complaints must be resolved fairly and clearly. The bank must explain what will happen next. They must state any actions they will take. They must correct errors. They must fix records. They must restore financial loss. They must take steps to prevent the issue happening again. Resolution is not simply the end of the process. It is the point at which the issue is put right.

These rights give you a strong position throughout the complaints process. When you understand your rights, you can respond with clarity. You can recognise when the bank has failed to follow the rules. You can challenge decisions effectively. You can direct the bank to the correct evidence. You can escalate when needed. Understanding your rights gives you the confidence to approach the process with structure and control.

Chapter 3

How to Make a Strong Stage One Complaint to Your Bank

A strong Stage One complaint gives the bank everything it needs to investigate your issue properly. Banks use a single stage formal complaint process, so the quality of your first complaint is important. It shapes the direction of the investigation, the information the bank looks for, and the clarity of the final response. When your complaint is clear, structured, and supported by evidence, you increase the chance of a fair outcome. This chapter explains how to prepare a strong complaint, how to organise your information, and how to describe your issue in a way that helps the bank carry out a thorough investigation.

Banks read complaints in a specific way. When a complaint arrives, the handler reviews the basic details first. They check your name, address, and account information. They check whether the complaint is new or linked to an earlier case. They look for a short description of the issue. They then review the notes on your account, the communication history, and the relevant records. If the complaint is unclear, the handler must guess what happened. This increases the chance of mistakes. A clear complaint reduces uncertainty and makes it easier for the bank to understand what went wrong.

A strong complaint starts with a simple introduction that explains the core issue. Many complaints begin with long descriptions that mix background information, frustration, and unclear detail. This makes the investigation harder. Your introduction should explain the basic problem in one or two sentences. For example, you might say that a payment was delayed, a card was blocked incorrectly, a charge was applied without explanation, or a transfer was lost. This gives the handler a clear starting point.

After the introduction, the next step is to describe the facts in a clear timeline. A timeline helps the handler understand what happened and when. Timelines reduce confusion, especially when several events occurred close together. When you write a timeline, start with the date and then write a short description of the event. Avoid emotional language. Focus on what happened. For example, if a card transaction was declined, explain the date, time, and location. If you received incorrect advice, say when the advice was given and what was said. When you provide a clear timeline, the handler knows which records to check.

Your complaint should also explain why the issue is wrong. This is an important part of a strong complaint. Many customers state that something went wrong but do not explain why it is unfair or incorrect. When you explain this clearly, you help the bank understand the impact of the error. For example, if a payment was delayed, explain that the delay caused a bill to be missed. If a charge was applied without explanation, explain that the charge does not match your account terms. If your account was blocked incorrectly, explain that you were unable to access your money. Explaining why the issue is wrong helps guide the investigation.

Evidence plays a major role in strong complaints. Banks rely on records, but they do not always gather all evidence unless you direct them to it. When you include evidence, you help the bank understand your case more clearly. Evidence can include screenshots, emails, letters, statements, or references to call recordings. When you refer to a call, provide the date and approximate time. This helps the handler locate the correct recording. When you provide evidence clearly, the bank can confirm facts more easily.

Another important part of a strong complaint is explaining the impact. Impact is not about describing how angry or stressed you felt. Impact refers to the practical effect of the issue. When the bank understands the impact, they can assess the seriousness of the issue. For example, if a delayed payment caused a missed bill, explain this. If a card block left you without access to money, explain where you were and what you were unable to do. If incorrect advice caused further problems, explain what those problems were. Impact is an important part of fair redress.

A strong complaint also includes a clear statement of what you want the bank to do. Many complaints fail because they do not include this information. When the bank understands what you want, they can focus the investigation. For example, you may ask the bank to review a charge, correct an error, investigate a payment, refund fees, or provide a clearer explanation. You may ask them to review a call recording or a transaction log. When you state this clearly, you help the bank understand your expectations.

Another part of strong complaint writing is keeping your language simple. Banks do not require complicated wording. Simple language helps the handler understand your point quickly. When language is complicated, vague, or emotional, the complaint becomes harder to follow. The strongest complaints use short sentences, clear points, and organised structure.

An effective structure for any bank complaint includes an introduction, a timeline, an explanation of why the issue is wrong, evidence, impact, and the action you want taken. This structure helps the bank investigate fairly and avoids misunderstandings. The bank can follow your points easily and check the correct records. A structured complaint shows that you understand the issue clearly, which encourages the bank to take your case seriously.

Clarity is important. When you write your complaint, avoid mixing several issues together. If more than one issue occurred, separate them into short sections. This helps the handler review each issue properly. Mixed complaints can lead to partial investigations, as the bank may focus on only one point. When your points are clear and separated, the investigation is more complete.

Another part of strong complaint writing is avoiding assumptions. Do not assume you know why something happened. Instead, describe what happened and ask the bank to explain the cause. When you avoid assumptions, you prevent the bank from focusing on the wrong issue. For example, do not assume that a payment was held due to fraud checks. Instead, state that the payment was held and ask the bank to confirm the reason. This helps ensure the investigation is based on facts rather than speculation.

Your complaint should also avoid unnecessary detail. Describe only the relevant events. Unrelated background information makes the complaint harder to follow and may distract the bank from the main issue. Keep your focus on the specific problem and the key dates, evidence, and impact.

Banks must acknowledge complaints within a reasonable time. This is part of your rights. When you submit a clear complaint, the acknowledgment is more likely to reflect the correct issue. If the acknowledgment does not match your complaint, you can respond and correct it. This helps the bank avoid misdirected investigations.

When you prepare a complaint, think about the records the bank will review. For example, if your complaint involves payments, the handler will check transaction logs. If it involves security issues, they will check security records. If it involves advice, they will check call notes and recordings. When you refer to the correct evidence, you direct the bank towards the right records. This strengthens your case.

Another important part of a strong complaint is accuracy. Check your dates. Check your times. Check the amounts. Incorrect dates or times can lead the bank to check the wrong records. This may result in incorrect conclusions. Taking time to ensure accuracy helps avoid these problems.

Banks must also follow the eight-week rule. When you submit a structured complaint, it becomes easier to track progress. If the bank does not send a final response by the end of the eighth week, you can escalate to the Financial Ombudsman Service. A clear complaint helps the Ombudsman understand your case more quickly. This increases the chance of a fair outcome.

Another reason structured complaints are effective is that they help the complaint handler understand the seriousness of the issue. When points are clear, evidence is easy to follow, and impact is described precisely, the investigation is more likely to be thorough. Structured complaints reduce the chance of misunderstanding and increase the chance of a fair decision.

A strong complaint also sets the tone for the rest of the process. When the bank sees that your complaint is organised and factual, they are more likely to investigate properly. It signals that you understand the process. It also helps prevent the bank from dismissing your concerns without proper explanation.

Writing a strong complaint does not require specialist knowledge. It requires clear thinking, accurate information, and a simple structure. When you follow the steps in this chapter, you give the bank what they need to investigate properly. The clearer your complaint, the easier it is to take the next step if their response is incomplete or unfair.

A strong complaint must also show that you understand what the bank should have done. This does not mean quoting every rule. It means explaining the basic expectation in simple terms. For example, if a payment was delayed, you can explain that the bank should process payments within a reasonable time. If advice was incorrect, you can explain that you rely on the bank to provide accurate information. If a charge was applied unfairly, you can explain that charges should reflect your account terms. This creates a clear link between what happened and what should have happened. When the bank sees this link, they are more likely to recognise the error.

Another important part of writing a strong complaint is distinguishing between facts and views. Facts are events, dates, and records. Views are opinions or interpretations. A clear complaint presents the facts first and then explains your view of why the issue is wrong. When facts and views are mixed together, the investigation can become confused. Keeping them separate helps the handler understand the situation clearly. It also helps if the complaint is later reviewed by the Ombudsman.

A strong complaint also explains what you did to try to resolve the issue before raising the complaint. This helps the bank see the full picture. If you contacted customer services, explain when and what they told you. If you visited a branch, explain what happened. If you were told to wait, explain how long you waited and what occurred next. This helps the handler understand whether staff gave incorrect advice or failed to act on your request.

Your complaint should always be factual and calm. Banks respond better to clear points than emotional language. This does not mean ignoring serious impact. It means describing that impact in a direct and specific way. For example, instead of saying that the issue caused major stress, you can explain the practical consequences that caused the stress. This improves the investigation because it links the emotional outcome to the specific events.

Another part of a strong complaint is explaining what information you are still missing. Many complaints arise because customers do not understand why something happened. If you did not receive a clear reason for a decision, say so. If you received conflicting information, explain this. If the explanation was incomplete, list the points that were unanswered. This tells the bank where their communication failed and what they need to address.

It is also important to keep your complaint focused on your experience. Avoid speculating about general policies or motives. Focus on what happened to you. The complaint handler will be able to compare your experience with the rules and policies that apply. When your complaint is focused on your actual experience, the investigation becomes clearer and more precise.

Another effective technique is to reference the correct internal record types. For example, you can ask the bank to check the payment log for the specific transaction. You can ask them to check the security events for the date your card was blocked. You can ask them to review the call recording from the date you received advice. You can ask them to check the direct debit record or the standing order instruction. This shows the handler exactly which records to review. It also reduces the chance of the handler reviewing the wrong evidence.

A strong complaint also makes it easier for the bank to identify whether the problem was caused by system issues, human error, or policy application. For example, if you were told different things by different advisers, that suggests human error or unclear records. If payments failed at the same time each day, that may suggest a system issue. If a decision matches an internal rule but conflicts with regulation, that may relate to policy. When your complaint is structured clearly, the handler is more likely to recognise the type of problem and review the correct area.

Your complaint should also challenge unclear or generic explanations. If the bank has previously given you an explanation that does not make sense, include this in your complaint. Explain why it was unclear. Ask the bank to provide a proper explanation. This helps focus the investigation and encourages the bank to address gaps in the earlier communication.

You should also consider the tone of your complaint. A calm and factual tone increases the chance of a clear, respectful response. When a complaint is hostile or aggressive, it can distract from the facts. It may cause staff to focus more on the tone than the substance. A clear, steady tone helps the handler concentrate on the evidence and the problem you are raising.

Another important part of strong complaint writing is anticipating the questions the handler will need to answer. Handlers will need to know what happened, why it happened, what should have happened, what the impact was, and what you want the bank to do. When your complaint answers these points, the handler can focus on the investigation instead of asking basic questions. This speeds up the process and improves the quality of the final response.

A strong complaint also makes clear distinctions between separate issues. If your issue involves more than one problem, separate them clearly. For example, if the bank blocked your card and also applied an incorrect charge, treat these as separate points. Explain each point in its own short section. This helps the bank address each issue properly. Mixing issues together can lead to incomplete responses.

You should also avoid unnecessary repetition. State each fact once. Repeating the same information can make the complaint harder to follow. Clear, concise points are easier for the handler to understand and investigate. This helps maintain a strong structure and prevents confusion.

Accuracy remains important throughout your complaint. If you are unsure about a date or time, say so. Do not guess. If you are not certain about the exact wording of advice you received, explain what you remember clearly and mention that it is based on memory. This helps the bank assess the reliability of your information and check the relevant records.

A strong complaint provides enough detail for the handler to understand the issue without overwhelming them with unnecessary information. Long descriptions that include unrelated background can make the complaint weaker. Stick to the relevant points. Explain what happened, when it happened, why it is wrong, what the impact was, and what you want the bank to do next.

You should also think about how the bank will verify the information you provide. Handlers rely on internal systems, so your complaint should help them locate the correct records. When you mention a call, provide the date and approximate time. When you mention a payment, provide the date, amount, and method. When you mention a branch visit, provide the location. This helps the handler find the evidence quickly and reduces the risk of mistakes.

A strong complaint also makes it easier to escalate the issue if needed. When your complaint is structured and clear, the Financial Ombudsman Service will be able to read it and understand the issue immediately. This increases the chance of a fair decision. It also helps the Ombudsman identify where the bank's investigation was incomplete or incorrect.

Another advantage of a strong complaint is that it helps prevent misunderstandings later in the process. When your points are clear, the bank cannot claim that they misunderstood your issue. This protects you from unfair or incomplete decisions. It also helps you challenge any statements in the final response that do not match what you originally wrote.

Your complaint should also highlight the most important points first. This helps the handler see the key issue quickly. Secondary points can come later in the structure. This approach ensures that the main issue receives proper attention.

A strong complaint also sets expectations. When you tell the bank what you want them to do, they must consider it. If they believe the request is unreasonable, they must explain why. This creates transparency and reduces confusion. It also helps the Ombudsman understand your expectations if you escalate the complaint later.

The goal of a strong complaint is not to overwhelm the handler with information. It is to provide a clear, accurate, and structured account of the issue. When you do this, you give the bank the best chance of resolving the issue fairly. You also prepare a strong foundation for the rest of the process.

A well written complaint improves the quality of the bank's investigation. When the handler understands the issue clearly, they can check the correct records. They can identify the correct team to contact. They can gather the correct information. Clear structure speeds up the process and reduces the chance of errors. This increases the chance of a fair outcome.

Writing a strong complaint empowers you. It helps you approach the process with confidence. It ensures your voice is heard. It reduces the chance of being ignored or dismissed. When you understand the structure and follow it carefully, you take control of the situation from the start.

Chapter 4
How to Assess Your Bank's Stage One Response

When you receive a Stage One response from your bank, your first task is to read it slowly and carefully. Many customers skim responses because they are long or because the issue has already caused frustration. This is understandable, but reading carefully is essential. A Stage One response tells you what the bank believes happened, what evidence they considered, what they did not consider, and how they reached their decision. It also tells you whether the bank has understood your complaint properly. This chapter explains how to assess the response in a clear and structured way, so you can decide whether the outcome is fair or whether you need to challenge it.

The first question to ask is whether the response addresses the complaint you actually raised. Banks sometimes respond to a different issue from the one you described. This can happen when the complaint was interpreted incorrectly or when the handler focused on one part of your message and ignored the rest. Compare the response with your original complaint. If the response does not match your complaint, this is a clear sign that the investigation may be incomplete. A fair response must address every point you raised. When the bank has misunderstood your complaint, you should prepare to challenge this.

Next, check whether the bank provided a clear summary of your complaint. A Stage One response should begin by explaining what the bank understands your complaint to be. This summary guides the rest of the investigation. If the summary is incomplete or inaccurate, the investigation may not cover all points. You have the right to expect an accurate summary. If the bank has misinterpreted your issue, you will need to correct this in your next communication.

The response should also explain what evidence the bank reviewed. This is a key part of the process. The bank should say which records they checked. These may include call recordings, transaction logs, security events, email communication, branch notes, online banking records, or internal logs. If the response does not mention evidence, this may indicate that the investigation was not thorough. A fair investigation must be based on evidence, not assumptions. When evidence is missing, the bank should explain why.

You should also check whether the response addresses each point of your complaint separately. A clear complaint contains several points: what happened, why it is wrong, the evidence, the impact, and what you want the bank to do. A fair response should address each point clearly. If the response only addresses the main issue but ignores the impact or ignores a secondary point, the investigation may be incomplete. The bank must review all parts of your complaint, not only the part that is easiest to address.

Another important part to assess is the reasoning behind the bank's decision. A fair response explains how the bank reached its conclusion. The reasoning should be clear and logical. You should be able to follow the explanation from the facts to the conclusion. If the reasoning is unclear, this may indicate that the investigation is incomplete or that the handler did not explain the decision properly. Vague explanations, generic phrases, or unclear statements weaken the quality of the response.

You should also look for signs that the bank relied too heavily on internal policy. Policies guide staff, but they are not the final authority. Banks must follow regulation. When a response relies only on internal policy without explaining how the policy fits with the rules, this may indicate a problem. A fair response refers to the correct rules when needed. For example, if the issue involves a direct debit, the response should consider the Direct Debit Guarantee. If the issue involves complaints handling, the response should follow the eight-week rule. If the issue involves unfair treatment, the response should consider the duty to treat customers fairly.

Another important part of assessing a response is checking whether the bank acknowledged any errors. When the bank has made a mistake, they should admit it clearly. A fair response explains what went wrong and how the error occurred. If the bank avoids admitting errors or provides explanations that do not match the facts, you can challenge this. Banks must not ignore evidence. When evidence shows an error, they must address it.

The response should also explain what the bank will do next. If they uphold the complaint, they should explain the steps they will take to put things right. This may include refunds, corrections to records, compensation, or updates to internal information. If the response does not explain the next steps, you may need to ask for clarification. A fair response must include clear actions.

Another key part is the explanation of redress. If the bank offers redress, they must explain the basis for the amount. They should explain whether the redress covers financial loss, inconvenience, distress, or a combination of these. If the amount seems too low or does not reflect the impact you described, you can challenge it. You have the right to ask the bank to explain how they calculated the amount.

You should also look for consistency. Check whether the response matches the evidence you provided. If you provided screenshots, emails, or statements, check whether the response reflects them accurately. If the bank's explanation does not match the evidence, this is a strong sign that the investigation was incomplete. Inconsistent explanations often indicate that the handler did not review the evidence properly.

Another important point is whether the bank addressed the timelines you provided. When you give dates and times, the investigation should review the events in the correct order. If the bank's explanation uses different dates or ignores key events, the response may not be reliable. Timelines are important because they help uncover delays, errors, or incorrect decisions. A fair response must reflect the timeline accurately.

You should also look for signs of generic wording. Banks often use templates when writing responses. Templates help maintain consistency, but they can weaken the quality of the investigation when used incorrectly. Generic wording includes phrases that do not relate to your case. If the response feels too general, it may indicate that the handler did not personalise the investigation. A fair response should reflect the details of your case.

Another important part of assessing a response is understanding whether the bank considered your circumstances. The rules require banks to take your situation into account. When you describe your circumstances in your complaint, the response should reflect this. If the response ignores your circumstances, this may indicate that the bank did not assess the case fairly. This is particularly important when financial difficulty, health issues, or other responsibilities are involved.

Your assessment should also consider whether the bank explained the cause of the issue. A clear response should state what caused the problem. If the cause is not explained, the response may be incomplete. For example, if a payment was delayed, the bank should explain whether the delay occurred before or after it left the bank. If advice was incorrect, the bank should explain what went wrong in the communication. Understanding the cause helps prevent the issue from happening again.

Another point to look for is whether the bank considered your evidence. If you submitted documents, screenshots, or information, the response should mention them. When evidence is ignored, the investigation is incomplete. A fair response should explain how the evidence influenced the decision.

You should also check whether the response reflects the full impact you described. If you explained that the issue caused financial loss or disrupted essential payments, the response should address this. If the response mentions the issue but ignores the impact, the outcome may not be fair. Impact is an important part of redress, and it must be considered.

The response should also explain your right to escalate the complaint. A fair response must include information about the Financial Ombudsman Service. It must explain that you can escalate the case once you receive the final response or once eight weeks pass. If the response does not include this information, it may not meet the required standards. This omission weakens the process and can be challenged.

Clarity is essential. When you read the response, ask yourself whether you understand it. If the explanation is confusing or contradictory, this may indicate poor investigation. A fair response should be easy to follow. It should not require interpretation. When a response is unclear, you have the right to request clarification.

You should also consider whether the outcome matches the evidence. Sometimes the evidence supports the complaint, but the bank rejects it. This may occur when the investigation was rushed or when the handler relied too heavily on internal assumptions. If the outcome does not match the facts, you should prepare to challenge the decision.

Another part of assessing a response is checking whether the bank provided correct information. When description of processes or policies appears incorrect, you can challenge this. Banks must give accurate information. Incorrect statements weaken the response and can be raised in the next stage.

You should also assess whether the bank considered all relevant parts of your complaint. If they addressed some points but not others, the investigation is incomplete. A fair response should cover every point you raised.

Another important point is whether the bank explained what they have learned from the complaint. Some responses include statements about improving processes or communication. These statements show that the bank understood the issue. When such statements are missing, the bank may have treated the complaint only as a formality.

A thorough assessment of the Stage One response helps you decide whether to accept the outcome or challenge it. When you understand how to assess the quality of the response, you can identify gaps, errors, and incomplete reasoning. This gives you the confidence to decide your next step.

Chapter 5

How to Challenge an Incomplete or Unfair Stage One Response

When you receive a Stage One response that feels incomplete or unfair, the next step is to challenge it in a clear and organised way. A poor response does not mean the bank has acted deliberately. It often means the handler did not investigate fully, did not understand your complaint clearly, or relied too heavily on assumptions. Challenging a weak response is an important part of the process, and the rules allow you to do this. Banks must consider your challenge fairly, and they must ensure their final decision reflects all relevant evidence.

The first step when challenging a poor response is to identify exactly what is wrong with it. This requires a careful reading. Many customers jump straight to frustration, but frustration does not help you identify the weaknesses in the investigation. Read the response slowly. Highlight parts that do not make sense. Highlight explanations that do not address your complaint. Highlight areas where evidence is missing. Highlight any contradictions. These markings form the basis of your challenge.

Your challenge must focus on specific points. When a response is vague or incomplete, you need to pinpoint what was missed. For example, if the bank did not address part of your timeline, you should state this clearly. If the response ignores your evidence, list the evidence again. If the reasoning does not follow the facts, explain where the explanation breaks down. Specific points help the handler understand what needs to be corrected. General statements such as "the response is unfair" do not help the investigation.

When the bank misinterprets your complaint, you must correct the misunderstanding directly. This is important because an incorrect interpretation leads to an incorrect investigation. Compare the response with your original complaint and identify where the misunderstanding occurred. Then provide a short and clear correction. For example, if the handler said that your complaint was about a charge, but your complaint was actually about incorrect advice, state that clearly. When the interpretation is corrected, the bank must investigate the correct issue.

You should also focus on missing evidence. Banks must check the correct records when investigating complaints. If the response does not mention a record that should have been reviewed, this is a clear weakness. For example, if you raised concerns about incorrect advice, the bank should listen to the relevant call. If you raised concerns about a failed payment, they should check the payment logs. If you raised concerns about a card block, they should check the security events. When a record is missing, you should identify it and ask the bank to review it. This helps ensure the next investigation is based on the correct information.

Your challenge should also address unclear or vague explanations. When banks provide vague explanations, it often means the handler did not have all the information or did not explain it clearly. If an explanation does not make sense, state this plainly. If the explanation does not answer your question, ask for a clearer one. You have the right to clear communication. When the explanation is unclear, the bank must provide a better one.

Another important part of challenging a poor response is pointing out contradictions. Contradictions appear when the bank gives conflicting explanations or when their explanation does not match the evidence. For example, if the bank says a payment was processed correctly but your statement shows a delay, this is a contradiction. If the bank says a call recording supports their decision but the summary does not match what you remember, this is another contradiction. When contradictions appear, list them clearly. Contradictions weaken the bank's position and require further investigation.

You should also challenge incomplete reviews. If the bank did not address all points in your complaint, you must highlight the missing parts. For example, the bank may have addressed the main issue but ignored the impact. They may have discussed a charge but ignored the incorrect advice that led to it. They may have looked at one payment but ignored another related event. When points are missing, state this clearly. A fair investigation must address every point.

Sometimes the bank will provide explanations that rely heavily on internal policy. Internal policy is not the final authority. It cannot override regulation. When the bank uses policy as the main justification, you should ask them to explain how the policy aligns with the regulatory rules. For example, if the issue involves direct debit, the bank must consider the Direct Debit Guarantee. If it involves complaints handling, they must follow the eight-week rule. When you understand the rules, you can challenge decisions that rely only on policy.

Another important part of challenging a poor response is explaining why the outcome is unfair. You should link the outcome to the facts and explain where the reasoning fails. For example, if the bank rejects your complaint about a card block, but the block was caused by incorrect information, explain this. If the bank rejects your complaint about incorrect advice, but the call recording shows that the advice was wrong, ask them to confirm whether they listened to the correct recording. When you highlight these gaps, you force the bank to respond to the actual issue.

Your challenge should also remind the bank of the impact, especially if the Stage One response did not consider it. Impact is important because it shapes redress. If the bank ignored the impact, you should restate it clearly. This helps the bank understand the seriousness of the issue and ensures the next investigation considers the full picture.

Another important part of challenging a response is clarity. Your challenge should follow a simple structure. Start by stating that you are challenging the response. Then list each issue separately. Use simple headings if needed. Keep your points focused on facts and evidence. Avoid emotional language. This structure helps the handler understand your points quickly and reduces the chance of misunderstandings.

Your challenge must also ask the bank to review specific information. When you direct the bank to the correct records, the investigation becomes more accurate. Banks sometimes check only surface level information. When you direct them to deeper evidence, they must review it. This helps prevent reliance on assumptions or incomplete information.

When challenging a poor response, you should also check whether the bank has met the correct standards for final responses. If the response does not include information about your right to escalate to the Financial Ombudsman Service, this is a weakness. If the response does not state clearly whether the complaint was upheld, partially upheld, or rejected, this is another weakness. If the response does not explain the reasoning behind the decision, it may not meet the regulatory standards. You can highlight these weaknesses in your challenge.

You should also highlight any delays that occurred. Banks must handle complaints within eight weeks. If the response took longer without explanation, this is relevant. If the bank missed updates or failed to acknowledge your complaint promptly, this is relevant. Delays can weaken the quality of the investigation and may justify escalation.

Another part of challenging a poor response is explaining what you want the bank to do. When you submit your challenge, you should state clearly what you expect from the next review. For example, you may ask them to review a specific call, check a specific log, correct an error, refund a charge, or provide a clearer explanation. A clear request helps the handler focus their next review.

The tone of your challenge is important. Keep it calm and factual. Focus on the issues, not frustration. A calm tone strengthens your argument. It helps the handler focus on the evidence and the gaps in the investigation. Tone does not affect your rights, but it can influence how well the handler understands your points.

Challenging a poor response is not about repeating your complaint. It is about identifying the weaknesses in the investigation and asking the bank to address them. When you challenge in a structured and factual way, you give the bank the information they need to carry out a proper review. It also strengthens your position if you later escalate to the Ombudsman.

You should also keep accurate records when challenging a response. Save the bank's response. Save your challenge. Save any evidence you submit. If you escalate to the Ombudsman later, these records will be important. The Ombudsman will review the full history. A clear record helps them understand where the investigation went wrong.

Understanding how to challenge a weak response gives you more control over the process. Banks must treat challenges seriously. They cannot ignore them. They must review the evidence properly. They must provide a clear explanation. When you understand how to challenge effectively, you improve the quality of the investigation and increase the chance of a fair outcome.

When preparing your challenge, it is useful to consider how the handler will approach the next review. They will return to your account records, the communication history, the transaction logs, and any policy documents that apply. They will re-read your complaint and then compare it with the points you raise in your challenge. This means your challenge should be structured in a way that mirrors how the handler will review the case. When your points follow a clear sequence, the investigation becomes easier for the bank to carry out accurately.

A clear challenge starts with a short summary that explains why you believe the response is incomplete or unfair. You do not need a long introduction. A single sentence that states the issue is enough. After the summary, list each concern as a separate point. When your points are separated, the handler can address them one by one. This prevents confusion and ensures the investigation covers everything. Many poor reviews occur because the handler misunderstood the structure of the challenge. A clear layout reduces this risk.

When addressing each concern, begin with what the bank claimed in their response. State the relevant part of the response and then explain why it is incorrect or incomplete. This helps the handler understand exactly which part of the response you are challenging. It also prevents the handler from assuming you are challenging other parts. Keeping the focus on the specific sections strengthens your position and increases clarity.

If the bank did not review evidence properly, you should point this out directly. You can explain which records you expected them to check and why they are relevant. For example, if you raised concerns about a failed payment, you can state that the bank did not review the payment logs. If the complaint involved incorrect advice, you can state that the relevant call recording was not mentioned. If the bank relied only on account notes without checking the recording, the investigation was incomplete. Being specific helps the handler understand where the original process failed.

Another useful technique is to quote short sections of the response when they contain errors. Quoting the exact wording helps the handler locate the incorrect explanation quickly. After quoting the wording, you can explain why it does not address your complaint or why it is factually incorrect. This prevents the handler from misunderstanding your points. It also shows that you read the response carefully, which encourages the handler to approach the next review with greater care.

When the bank provides an explanation that conflicts with your evidence, point out the conflict clearly. You can explain what your evidence shows and why it contradicts the explanation. When conflicts are clear, the handler must resolve them. They cannot ignore evidence that disproves their earlier explanation. Banks must base their decisions on facts. When you highlight a contradiction, you strengthen your position and encourage a more thorough review.

If the bank explains the issue using general statements rather than the facts of your case, highlight this. Many poor responses rely on generic wording. This wording may explain general processes rather than what actually happened. When responses rely on templates, they often miss key details. You can explain that the response uses general statements without addressing the specific events in your complaint. This encourages the handler to look at the facts instead of relying on templates.

Your challenge should also address any parts of the response that feel incomplete. Incomplete responses may fail to explain the cause of the issue. They may fail to explain what evidence was reviewed. They may fail to address the impact. They may ignore important dates. When you identify incomplete sections, explain why they are incomplete and state what information is missing. This helps the handler understand the gaps that must be filled during the next review.

If the bank's explanation does not follow a logical sequence, you can challenge the reasoning. Explain where the reasoning breaks down and why it does not reflect the facts. If the reasoning skips important steps or relies on assumptions, state this. When the reasoning is flawed, the conclusion may also be flawed. A clear explanation of the flaws helps the handler understand where they must reevaluate the decision.

When the bank relied on incorrect dates or times, highlight the correct ones. Incorrect dates weaken the quality of the investigation. They may cause the handler to review the wrong evidence. When you correct the dates, you help the next handler look at the correct records. You can also explain how the incorrect dates affected the original investigation. This improves the accuracy of the next review.

If the bank did not consider the impact, restate it clearly. Impact is an important part of fair redress. When the bank ignores the impact, the outcome may not reflect the seriousness of the issue. Restating the impact helps the handler understand what was missed. Keep the impact factual and specific. This helps the bank understand the real effect of the problem.

Your challenge should also address any sections where the bank's explanation is inconsistent with earlier communication. If you were given certain information by staff and the response contradicts it, explain this clearly. Inconsistent communication is a strong indicator that the investigation was incomplete. When you highlight inconsistencies, the handler must review the earlier communication and resolve any conflicts. This helps ensure the next investigation is based on accurate information.

Another part of challenging a poor response is addressing situations where the bank failed to follow the correct rules. If the issue involves direct debit, the bank must follow the Direct Debit Guarantee. If the issue involves complaints handling, they must follow the eight-week rule. If the issue involves incorrect advice, they must consider their duty to provide accurate information. If the issue involves unfair treatment, they must consider the duty to treat customers fairly. When you explain which rule applies and why it matters, you help the handler understand their obligations.

You should also address cases where the bank did not consider your circumstances. Many responses focus only on the technical details and ignore the human impact. If you explained your circumstances in your complaint and the bank ignored them, state this clearly. Banks must consider individual circumstances. When they fail to do so, the investigation may not reflect the full picture. Highlighting this strengthens your challenge.

Another important part of challenging a poor response is requesting the correct next steps. You should ask the bank to conduct a full review of the points you identified. You can ask them to check specific records. You can ask them to explain the cause more clearly. You can ask them to consider the impact. You can ask them to correct errors. A clear request helps the handler understand what you expect from the next review.

Your challenge should also state that you expect a clear and complete response. This encourages the bank to focus on clarity and accuracy. A clear expectation reduces the chance of another incomplete investigation. When you state your expectations calmly and clearly, the bank is more likely to take your case seriously.

You should keep your challenge organised. Use short sections or headings if needed. This helps the handler understand your points quickly. Organisation improves clarity and reduces the risk of misunderstandings. A disorganised challenge may cause the handler to focus on the wrong points.

Your tone should remain calm and factual. Anger and frustration are understandable, but they do not help the investigation. A calm tone strengthens your points. It makes the handler more likely to approach the next review with care and respect. Tone does not change your rights, but it affects the clarity of communication.

You should also keep accurate records when submitting your challenge. Save your challenge, the bank's response, and any additional evidence you provide. These records will be important if you later escalate the case. The Financial Ombudsman Service reviews the full complaint history. Clear records help the Ombudsman understand what went wrong during the Stage One investigation.

Challenging a poor response is part of the process. Banks do not always get things right. Investigations can be rushed, and staff can misunderstand complaints. When you challenge a poor response in a clear and structured way, you help the bank conduct a proper review. You also prepare a strong foundation if you later need to escalate your case to the Ombudsman.

A strong challenge increases the chance of a fair outcome. It ensures the bank looks at the correct evidence. It helps correct misunderstandings. It provides clarity. It strengthens your position. It gives you control. When you understand how to challenge an incomplete or unfair response, you approach the process with confidence and structure.

Chapter 6

How Banks Conduct Stage One Investigations

A Stage One investigation is the bank's first formal review of your complaint. It is the point at which the bank gathers information, checks records, and compares your account of events with their internal evidence. Many customers assume that banks carry out detailed investigations automatically, but this is not always the case. Some investigations are thorough and accurate. Others rely on limited information. Understanding how banks conduct Stage One investigations helps you recognise when the process is fair and when important steps have been missed.

Banks begin a Stage One investigation by reviewing the complaint summary. This summary guides the investigation. It shapes what evidence the handler looks for, which teams they contact, and which records they examine. If the summary is inaccurate or incomplete, the investigation starts from the wrong point. This is why clear complaint writing is important. When the bank understands the issue correctly, the investigation is more likely to cover the correct events.

After reviewing the summary, the handler checks your account details. They confirm your identity, your account status, and any relevant account features. They check whether you have raised related complaints before. They may review previous decisions to understand whether the issue has occurred more than once. They may also check whether you have been given specific advice in earlier interactions. This helps them understand the context of the complaint.

The next step is to review internal notes. Banks record notes on nearly every interaction. These notes include brief summaries of calls, branch visits, online enquiries, and internal decisions. Notes help the handler understand what has been recorded so far. However, notes are not always detailed. Some advisers write short summaries that miss important information. Some notes are incomplete. Some are written quickly. When notes are unclear, the investigation may rely on assumptions. This is one reason why clear complaint structure is important. It helps correct gaps in the internal record.

After reviewing notes, the handler checks transaction records. These records show payments, charges, card usage, transfers, and other financial movements. Transaction logs contain more detail than customer statements. They show the precise time a payment was attempted, whether it was approved, whether it was declined, and why. They show the authorisation method used. They show whether fraud checks were triggered. When the complaint involves payments, a thorough investigation requires a detailed review of these logs. If the handler only looks at basic statements, the investigation will be incomplete.

Banks also review security logs when a complaint involves account access, card blocks, unusual activity, or login issues. Security logs show which devices were used, when login attempts occurred, whether any attempts failed, and whether internal security rules were triggered. These logs are detailed but can only be accessed by certain teams. If the handler does not consult the correct team, they may not see the full security history. This can lead to incorrect explanations, especially when account restrictions were applied automatically.

Another important part of Stage One investigations is reviewing call recordings. Banks record many calls, though not all. When a complaint involves incorrect advice, poor service, or conflicting information, reviewing the call recording is essential. However, handlers do not always listen to recordings unless you refer to them clearly. If the handler relies only on notes, important details may be missed. This is why clear complaints that reference specific calls, dates, and times improve the investigation. They guide the handler to the correct recordings.

Banks may also contact specialist teams when the issue involves fraud, chargebacks, mortgages, loans, or international transfers. Specialist teams have access to detailed records that frontline staff cannot view. These teams use their own systems, which store information differently. If the complaint requires specialist knowledge but the handler does not consult the correct team, the investigation may rely on incomplete information. Understanding this helps you recognise when a poor response may reflect a shallow investigation.

Another step in Stage One investigations is reviewing internal policy documents. Policies guide staff in how to handle different types of enquiries. They explain processes, timelines, and responsibilities. Policies can support fair decisions when used correctly. However, policies must follow regulation. When the handler relies solely on policy without comparing it to the regulatory rules, the investigation may be flawed. This is particularly important in areas such as direct debit, where regulation is strict. When you know the correct rules, you can challenge any part of the investigation that relies only on policy.

After gathering evidence, the handler compares your account of events with the records. They look for consistency, contradictions, and gaps. They assess whether the records support your description or the bank's earlier explanation. They consider the tone of communication, the timing of events, and any information that may have influenced the outcome. A thorough review requires the handler to consider all available evidence. When evidence is missing or ignored, the investigation becomes weaker.

Banks must also consider your circumstances. This is part of their duty to treat customers fairly. If you described financial difficulty, health challenges, or other circumstances in your complaint, the handler must consider these when reviewing the case. Circumstances can affect how the bank should have acted. For example, delays may have a greater impact when financial difficulty is present. Incorrect advice may be more harmful when the customer relied on it in a vulnerable situation. A fair investigation considers these factors.

Another part of Stage One investigations is reviewing communication history. This includes emails, secure messages, and branch notes. Communication history shows whether the bank provided correct information, responded within reasonable timeframes, or took appropriate steps. When the bank fails to review communication history, their understanding of the case becomes incomplete. Clear complaints that reference communication help guide the handler to the correct records.

Banks must also check whether staff followed internal processes correctly. Staff may have followed the wrong process, applied a rule incorrectly, or misinterpreted information. When process errors occur, the handler must identify them. Staff mistakes do not make the customer responsible. A fair investigation requires the handler to review whether staff actions influenced the outcome.

Another part of investigations is checking whether the system behaved as expected. Many issues arise from system behaviour. Systems may delay payments, flag transactions incorrectly, or misread information. When the complaint involves system issues, the handler must review system behaviour. This often requires input from technical teams. If technical teams are not consulted, the investigation may rely on assumptions rather than accurate information.

Once the handler gathers all evidence, they must assess whether the bank acted fairly. Fairness is not only about rules. It includes whether the bank considered your circumstances, communicated clearly, responded promptly, and treated you with respect. The duty to treat customers fairly means the handler cannot rely solely on technical explanations. They must consider the overall impact.

The handler must then write the response. A fair response explains the evidence reviewed, the reasoning behind the decision, and what the bank will do next. If the response is rushed, unclear, or incomplete, it usually means the investigation was not conducted properly. A good investigation produces a clear and structured response. When the response does not meet this standard, the bank must review the case again.

Understanding how Stage One investigations work helps you recognise whether the handler followed the correct steps. When you know the process, you can identify when evidence was missed, when explanations are incomplete, and when important details were ignored. This knowledge helps you challenge poor responses effectively and gives you confidence when deciding whether to escalate the case.

Chapter 7
How to Prepare for Escalation to the Financial Ombudsman Service

Escalating a complaint to the Financial Ombudsman Service is a significant step, and preparation is important. The Ombudsman will review the bank's investigation, your complaint, your evidence, the communication history, and the final response. They will assess whether the bank acted fairly. They will check whether the bank followed the rules. They will review the impact and decide what a fair outcome should be. Preparing for escalation does not mean rewriting your complaint. It means organising your information clearly so that the Ombudsman can understand the case quickly and without confusion. A well-prepared escalation increases the chance of a fair and accurate decision.

The first part of preparing for escalation is understanding when you are entitled to escalate. You have the right to take your case to the Ombudsman once the bank issues a final response or once eight weeks pass from the date the bank received your complaint. This rule protects you from delays. It prevents the bank from controlling the timeline indefinitely. If the bank takes longer than eight weeks without issuing a final response, you do not need to wait. You can escalate immediately. When the bank issues a final response, you have six months to take the complaint to the Ombudsman. If you wait longer, the Ombudsman may not be able to review the case unless there are exceptional circumstances.

Once you are entitled to escalate, the next step is to gather the relevant documents. These documents form the foundation of your escalation. The Ombudsman needs to see the original complaint, the bank's final response, any interim responses, any evidence you provided, and any communication that is relevant to the issue. You do not need to gather every message you ever sent. Focus on the material that explains the issue clearly. The goal is to present a clean and organised history of what happened. This helps the Ombudsman understand your case without having to interpret incomplete information.

Your first document is the original complaint. This shows how you described the issue, the timeline, the evidence, and the impact. It shows whether the bank correctly understood the issue. The Ombudsman will compare your complaint with the bank's response to see whether the bank addressed each point properly. When your original complaint is clear, this comparison becomes easy. If the bank misinterpreted your complaint, the Ombudsman will recognise this quickly.

Your second document is the final response from the bank. This response explains the bank's position. It shows the reasoning, the evidence reviewed, and the outcome. The Ombudsman will examine this response carefully. They will check whether the reasoning is clear. They will check whether the evidence supports the decision. They will check whether the bank followed the correct rules. They will check whether the bank addressed each point. A clear and accurate final response supports the bank's position. A vague or incomplete final response weakens it.

Your third set of documents includes any evidence you provided to the bank. Evidence can include screenshots, letters, emails, statements, or records showing the timeline. If you referred to a call recording, the Ombudsman may listen to it if the bank includes it in their file. The Ombudsman may also ask the bank to provide call recordings if they are relevant. Evidence helps the Ombudsman understand what happened, so it must be organised properly. Group similar evidence together. For example, group screenshots by date, group statements by month, and group emails by subject. This helps the Ombudsman follow the sequence without confusion.

Your fourth set of documents includes any communication between you and the bank that is relevant to the issue. This may include branch interactions, secure messages, or customer service responses. Only include communication that directly explains what happened. Irrelevant communication distracts from the main points. The Ombudsman values clarity. Presenting only what matters helps keep the focus on the issue.

Once you have gathered the documents, the next step is to write a clear escalation summary. This summary explains why you believe the bank's decision is wrong or incomplete. A good summary is short and factual. It is not a repeat of your original complaint. It is an explanation of the gaps in the bank's investigation. This summary guides the Ombudsman through the case. It shows the key issues that must be addressed during the review.

The escalation summary should begin with a short introduction that states the basic issue. This introduction is not a long narrative. It is a simple explanation of what went wrong. After the introduction, list your key points. Each point should explain a specific problem with the bank's investigation. Examples include missing evidence, incorrect reasoning, contradictions, incomplete explanations, or failure to follow the rules. When points are clear, the Ombudsman can review each one separately. This helps keep the investigation structured.

One important part of the summary is explaining which evidence the bank failed to review. The Ombudsman will not assume the bank checked everything. They will rely on the information in the bank's file. If your summary shows that the bank avoided reviewing call recordings, payment logs, or security events, the Ombudsman may request these records. This strengthens your case. The Ombudsman values evidence-based review. When your summary identifies gaps, the Ombudsman can address them directly.

Another important part is explaining why the bank's reasoning is flawed. You do not need legal language. A simple explanation is enough. For example, if the bank said a payment was not delayed but the evidence shows a delay, state this clearly. If the bank said advice was correct but the recording shows incorrect information, explain this. If the bank ignored your circumstances, state this. Reasoning errors weaken the bank's position. The Ombudsman reviews reasoning carefully. A clear summary helps them identify mistakes quickly.

Your summary should also include a short explanation of the impact. The Ombudsman considers both financial loss and inconvenience. Impact helps explain the seriousness of the issue. When you describe the impact clearly, the Ombudsman understands why the bank's decision may not be fair. Keep the explanation factual. Describe what happened, what it caused, and how it affected you. This strengthens your case without exaggeration.

Another part of preparation is organising your documents in a simple and clear order. The Ombudsman receives many files. When your file is organised, the Ombudsman can review it more easily. Clear organisation improves the quality of the review. It also shows that you understand the process, which encourages the Ombudsman to take your case seriously.

The final part of preparation is understanding the Ombudsman's approach. The Ombudsman is independent. They will not take the bank's side. They will not take your side. They will look at the facts. They will check whether the bank acted fairly. They will check whether the bank followed the rules. They will assess whether the outcome was reasonable. Knowing this helps you understand what the Ombudsman will look for. They will not be influenced by emotion or long narratives. They rely on clarity, evidence, and fairness.

Once you understand how the Ombudsman works, your next step is to prepare the information in a form that is easy for them to review. The Ombudsman deals with thousands of complaints every year, so clarity is essential. Your goal is not to overwhelm them with detail. Your goal is to present the facts in a clean and logical sequence. This helps the Ombudsman understand the issue quickly and prevents your case from becoming confused with unnecessary information.

Begin by organising your documents into groups. These groups help the Ombudsman navigate your file without wasting time. The first group should contain your original complaint and any written challenges you made to the bank's response. This material forms the foundation of your case. It shows the Ombudsman how you first explained the issue, how you structured your points, and how the bank's investigation developed.

The second group should contain the bank's responses. This includes the acknowledgment, any updates, and the final response. If the bank issued an interim response explaining that they needed more time, include this as well. These letters show how the bank handled the complaint. They show whether the bank met the eight-week rule. They show whether the bank explained the investigation properly. They show whether the bank followed the correct rules when making decisions.

The third group should contain your evidence. Evidence is important because it shows the Ombudsman the factual foundation of your case. When organising your evidence, place the most relevant items first. For example, if screenshots show the problem clearly, place them at the top of the group. If statements show delays or incorrect entries, place them next. If emails confirm incorrect advice, place them next. This arrangement gives the Ombudsman a clear path through the facts. Avoid repeating evidence. The Ombudsman only needs to see each piece once.

The fourth group should contain communication that supports your case. This may include chat logs, secure messages, branch notes, or email exchanges. Only include communication that relates directly to the issue. Irrelevant communication distracts from the main points and weakens the clarity of your submission. The Ombudsman values clean and focused information. Keeping only what matters strengthens the quality of your case.

Once your documents are grouped, the next step is to write a short cover message. This message is not a long description. It is a simple explanation of what you are sending and why you are escalating the complaint. The message should include four elements: the date the bank received your complaint, the date of the final response (or confirmation that eight weeks have passed), a short explanation of the issue, and a brief statement about why the bank's response is incomplete or unfair. This helps the Ombudsman understand immediately why you are seeking their help.

The next step is to write your escalation summary. This summary should be organised into clear sections. The first section explains what went wrong. The second section explains why the bank's investigation was incomplete. The third section explains why the outcome is unfair. The fourth section lists the evidence the bank failed to review. The fifth section explains the impact. A structured summary helps the Ombudsman review the case without confusion. They can follow each part of your reasoning and compare it to the bank's explanation.

When writing the summary, avoid emotional language. The Ombudsman focuses on facts, evidence, fairness, and clarity. Emotional statements may distract from the main points. Keep your sentences short and direct. Focus on what happened. Focus on what should have happened. Focus on what the evidence shows. The goal is to present a clear and stable account of the issue.

Your summary should never contradict your earlier letters. Consistency matters because it helps the Ombudsman trust the structure of your case. If the Ombudsman sees conflicting statements, they may have to request clarification. This slows the process and may weaken the clarity of the investigation. Stick to the facts. Stick to the evidence. Stick to your original structure.

Another part of preparation is anticipating the bank's defence. When the Ombudsman asks the bank for their file, the bank will provide their internal notes, the call recordings, relevant logs, and an explanation of their position. If you can anticipate what the bank might say, you can prepare your summary more effectively. For example, if the bank is likely to rely on internal policy, ask the Ombudsman to check whether the policy aligns with the correct rules. If the bank is likely to claim that notes reflect correct advice, explain why the call recording is important. Anticipating the bank's approach helps you prepare a stronger submission.

Another important step is checking the timeline. Timelines help reveal delays, errors, and gaps in the bank's investigation. The Ombudsman relies heavily on timelines because they provide a clear picture of how events unfolded. A clear timeline helps the Ombudsman understand whether the bank acted promptly, whether their explanation matches the sequence of events, and whether they missed important steps. When your timeline is accurate, it strengthens the clarity of your case.

It is also important to check whether the bank followed the correct rules. The Ombudsman will assess whether the bank followed the Financial Conduct Authority's principles, rules, and guidance. These include the duty to treat customers fairly, obligations around communication, rules regarding suitability of advice, rules regarding payment processing, and rules regarding complaint handling. If the bank failed to follow any of these rules, your escalation summary should highlight this. Clear references to rule breaches help the Ombudsman understand the seriousness of the issue.

Another part of preparation is considering what outcome you believe would be fair. A fair outcome depends on the facts of the case. You may want a refund of charges, a correction to your statements, compensation for inconvenience, or an explanation of what went wrong. You do not need to demand a specific amount. You only need to explain what type of redress would resolve the issue. This helps the Ombudsman understand the purpose of your escalation.

Once your preparation is complete, the final step is to submit the case to the Ombudsman. You can do this online, by phone, or by post. Online submission is the most efficient because you can attach documents easily and keep track of the case. When you submit your file, ensure each document is clear and readable. Poor quality scans or unclear screenshots may slow the investigation. The Ombudsman relies on clarity. Clear documents support a smooth review.

After submission, the Ombudsman will assign the case to an investigator. The investigator will review your file, the bank's file, and the communication history. They may ask you for more information if something is unclear. They may ask the bank for additional evidence. They will try to resolve the issue informally first. If an informal resolution is not possible, the case may proceed to an Ombudsman decision. This is the final stage. The decision is binding on the bank if you accept it.

Preparing for escalation is about clarity, structure, and evidence. When you follow these steps, you give the Ombudsman the information they need to assess your case fairly. You also give yourself a strong foundation for the next stage of the process. Preparation helps you stay in control and ensures the Ombudsman has a clear understanding of the issue from the start.

Chapter 8

What the Financial Ombudsman Service Looks For When Reviewing Your Complaint

When the Financial Ombudsman Service reviews your complaint, they follow a structured approach designed to reach a fair and reasonable outcome. Their role is different from the bank's role. They are not interested in defending the bank or supporting the customer by default. Their job is to look at what happened and decide what is fair. Understanding what the Ombudsman looks for gives you a clear advantage when preparing your escalation. It helps you focus on the strongest points and avoid unnecessary detail. It also helps you understand how the Ombudsman forms decisions and what evidence matters most.

The first thing the Ombudsman looks for is a clear understanding of your complaint. They need to know exactly what the issue is, how it happened, and how it affected you. They read your original complaint carefully. They check whether the complaint explains the timeline of events. They check whether you provided evidence. They check whether you described the impact. They check whether you were clear about what went wrong. A clear complaint helps the Ombudsman understand the starting point of the case. If the complaint is unclear, they will still work to understand it, but the process may take longer because the investigator must interpret what you meant.

The Ombudsman also looks at how the bank interpreted your complaint. Banks create an internal summary when they receive a complaint. That summary guides the investigation. The Ombudsman compares your original complaint with the bank's summary. If the summary does not match your complaint, it may indicate that the bank misunderstood the issue. A misunderstanding at the beginning can lead to an incomplete investigation. The Ombudsman takes this seriously because incorrect interpretation affects the entire process.

The next thing the Ombudsman examines is how the bank investigated the complaint. They expect the bank to check the correct evidence. They expect the bank to review transaction logs, security events, call recordings, communication history, and other relevant records. They expect the bank to contact specialist teams if needed. They expect the bank to follow the rules. When the bank's investigation is shallow or incomplete, the Ombudsman notices. They may ask the bank to provide more evidence or explain why certain records were not reviewed.

The Ombudsman checks whether the bank reviewed the complaint fairly and within the rules. Banks must follow the Financial Conduct Authority's principles, rules, and guidance. This includes the duty to treat customers fairly, the requirement to provide correct information, the requirement to handle complaints within eight weeks, and the requirement to explain decisions clearly. The Ombudsman compares the bank's actions with these rules. They check whether the bank acted reasonably. They check whether the bank's processes were followed properly. They check whether the bank communicated clearly. When the bank fails to follow the rules, this often strengthens the customer's case.

Another thing the Ombudsman examines is whether the bank considered the full sequence of events. Complaints often involve several steps, not a single incident. For example, a delayed payment may lead to a missed bill. A blocked card may cause practical difficulty in everyday life. Incorrect advice may cause financial loss later. The Ombudsman looks for a complete review. If the bank focused only on a single event and ignored the consequences, the investigation may not be fair. The Ombudsman expects banks to consider the whole picture.

The Ombudsman also checks how the bank evaluated the evidence. Banks hold detailed records, but not all investigations use these records properly. The Ombudsman looks at the evidence the bank reviewed and checks whether it supports the decision. For example, if the bank said that a payment was processed correctly, the Ombudsman checks the transaction logs. If the bank said the advice was correct, the Ombudsman checks the call recording. If the bank said the security block was justified, the Ombudsman checks the security logs. If the evidence does not support the bank's explanation, the Ombudsman can overturn the decision.

Another important part of the Ombudsman's review is the bank's reasoning. A fair response must explain why the bank reached its decision. The Ombudsman checks whether the reasoning is clear, logical, and based on evidence. If the reasoning relies on assumptions or contains contradictions, this is a sign of poor investigation. The Ombudsman does not accept unclear explanations. When the reasoning is weak, the Ombudsman may reject the bank's position and request a new review.

The Ombudsman also checks whether the bank addressed every point in your complaint. A fair response must consider each part. If you raised several issues and the bank ignored some of them, the response is incomplete. The Ombudsman checks for missing points by comparing your complaint with the bank's response. Missing points weaken the reliability of the decision and often lead to further review.

The Ombudsman also examines whether the bank considered your circumstances. Circumstances matter because they influence how the bank should have acted. If you were in financial difficulty, the bank should have taken extra care. If health issues affected your ability to manage your account, the bank should have communicated clearly. If the bank ignored your circumstances, the Ombudsman may consider this a breach of fairness. Circumstances help explain the seriousness of the issue and the impact it had. The Ombudsman takes this seriously.

Another thing the Ombudsman looks at is the impact of the issue. Impact includes financial loss, practical difficulty, inconvenience, and stress caused by the situation. The Ombudsman checks whether the bank considered the impact properly. Banks sometimes focus only on technical details. They may say that the correct process was followed but ignore the real effect on the customer. The Ombudsman balances both the technical and human side of the complaint. They consider what is reasonable in the circumstances. If the bank ignored the impact, the Ombudsman may decide that the outcome was not fair.

The Ombudsman also checks whether the bank acted within reasonable timeframes. Timeliness is an important part of fair service. Banks must acknowledge complaints, provide updates if needed, and issue final responses within eight weeks. If the bank delayed the investigation without explanation, this reflects poorly on their handling of the complaint. While delays do not automatically mean the outcome is wrong, they can indicate a lack of care. The Ombudsman may comment on delays and consider them when deciding fairness.

Another important factor is communication. The Ombudsman checks whether the bank communicated clearly during the investigation. They check whether the bank explained what they were doing. They check whether the bank answered questions properly. They check whether the final response was clear. If the bank's communication was confusing or misleading, this can reflect poor service. Poor communication may not change the technical outcome, but it affects fairness. The Ombudsman considers this when assessing the case.

The Ombudsman also checks whether the bank provided correct information during the issue. Incorrect information is a common cause of complaints. If the bank gave misleading or unclear advice, the Ombudsman takes this seriously. The accuracy of information matters because customers rely on the bank's explanations to make decisions. If the bank gave incorrect information and this caused an issue, the Ombudsman may order the bank to put things right.

When reviewing the evidence, the Ombudsman checks for contradictions. Contradictions between records, explanations, and outcomes are important. If the bank says one thing but the records show another, the Ombudsman will not accept the bank's explanation. They will rely on the evidence. Contradictions can reveal errors, incomplete reviews, or misunderstandings. The Ombudsman uses contradictions to test the strength of the bank's case.

The Ombudsman also checks whether the bank accepted responsibility when appropriate. When the bank made a mistake, they should acknowledge it. If the bank avoids admitting errors even when the evidence is clear, the Ombudsman may view the response as incomplete. Accepting responsibility is part of treating customers fairly. When banks refuse to acknowledge errors, this often weakens their position.

Another factor is whether the bank offered fair redress. Redress is an important part of the Ombudsman's review. The Ombudsman checks whether the bank offered an appropriate remedy. This may include refunds, corrections, compensation for inconvenience, or steps to prevent the issue from happening again. If redress is too low or missing, the Ombudsman may require the bank to provide more. Redress must reflect the impact and the seriousness of the issue.

The Ombudsman also checks whether the bank's explanation is consistent with industry rules. Industry rules include card scheme requirements, direct debit rules, and payment regulations. The Ombudsman checks whether the bank applied the rules correctly. If the bank misinterpreted a rule or relied on policy instead of regulation, the Ombudsman may overturn the decision. Industry rules exist to protect customers. When banks ignore them, the Ombudsman intervenes.

Finally, the Ombudsman considers fairness. Fairness is broader than rules. It includes how the bank acted, how they communicated, and how they responded to your circumstances. Fairness looks at what is reasonable in the situation. The Ombudsman uses fairness to balance the technical and practical sides of the issue. This approach ensures that the outcome reflects both the rules and the real impact on your life.

When the Ombudsman begins their detailed review, they build a full picture of what happened. They do not rely on a single document or one version of events. They look at everything together. This includes your complaint, your evidence, the bank's notes, the call recordings, the communication history, and the final response the bank issued. They compare each piece to see whether the information is consistent. If something does not fit, the Ombudsman explores it further. This layered approach helps them reach a conclusion that reflects both the technical and practical reality of the situation.

A central part of the Ombudsman's method is reviewing the communication trail. Communication shows how the issue unfolded in real time. It shows whether the bank responded promptly, whether they provided accurate information, and whether they took your concerns seriously. Many complaints involve misunderstandings or gaps in communication. The Ombudsman checks whether the bank gave clear explanations. If the communication was confusing, incomplete, or inconsistent, this affects the fairness of the bank's final decision. Communication failures are taken seriously because they often contribute to the problem.

Alongside communication, the Ombudsman pays close attention to recorded calls. Call recordings are highly valuable because they show the exact wording used by staff. They show whether the adviser gave correct information. They show whether the adviser understood your question. They show whether the adviser explained your options clearly. Call notes can never replace a recording. Notes may be vague or incomplete. The Ombudsman listens to the actual calls whenever they are relevant. If the bank did not listen to a recording, but it is important to the case, the Ombudsman identifies this as a gap in the investigation. When a call recording contradicts the bank's version of events, the Ombudsman relies on the recording, not the bank's notes.

The Ombudsman also checks transaction logs and technical records. These records show how the bank's systems behaved. Logs reveal whether payments were delayed, declined, queued, or processed correctly. They show whether a card block was triggered by system rules or staff intervention. They show whether the customer attempted a transaction multiple times. They show the exact moment a payment left the account. When the bank provides an explanation about a payment, the Ombudsman checks the logs to confirm accuracy. If the logs show a different story, the Ombudsman will not accept the bank's explanation.

Security logs are another important source of evidence. Complaints involving blocked cards, login problems, suspected fraud, or frozen accounts require detailed review of security records. Security logs show failed login attempts, security triggers, device information, and unusual activity. If the bank claims that a security rule was triggered, the Ombudsman checks the log to confirm whether this is true. If the log does not support the bank's explanation, the Ombudsman can reject the decision. When banks rely on vague security statements without showing the underlying records, the Ombudsman treats this as weak evidence.

Another part of the Ombudsman's analysis is reviewing how the bank applied its own processes. Banks must follow internal procedures that reflect FCA rules. The Ombudsman checks whether staff followed the correct process. If a process was skipped, ignored, or applied incorrectly, the investigation becomes unreliable. Process failures can include failing to escalate a problem, failing to follow up, failing to check the right records, or failing to follow mandatory checks. When process failures contributed to the issue, the Ombudsman takes this into account when deciding fairness.

Fairness is central to everything the Ombudsman does. Fairness means more than technical compliance. It involves considering the full situation. The Ombudsman asks whether the bank acted reasonably. They ask whether the bank should have done more. They ask whether the customer was treated with care. They ask whether the outcome reflects the real impact. Fairness includes recognising the effect of delays, errors, incorrect information, and communication failures. It also includes recognising the customer's circumstances. The Ombudsman does not view fairness as a rigid formula. They look at the whole picture and decide what is reasonable.

Another part of fairness is how the bank responded to the impact. The Ombudsman looks for signs that the bank understood the effect of the issue. They check whether the bank acknowledged the inconvenience or financial loss. They check whether the bank offered appropriate redress. If the bank ignored the impact or minimised it, the Ombudsman can challenge the adequacy of the outcome. The Ombudsman expects banks to recognise the practical effects of their mistakes. They expect banks to take responsibility for consequences, not only technical causes.

The Ombudsman also looks at whether the bank's explanation evolved during the process. Sometimes banks change their explanation when they realise the first explanation was weak. If explanations change without clear reason, the Ombudsman becomes cautious. They check whether the new explanation is supported by evidence. If explanations shift in a way that appears inconsistent, the Ombudsman may view this as a sign of incomplete investigation.

Another aspect of the Ombudsman's review is how the bank responded to your questions. If you asked the bank to explain something and they ignored the question, this affects the fairness of the process. If you asked the bank to check specific evidence and they refused without reason, this affects the quality of the investigation. If the bank dismissed your points without explanation, the Ombudsman considers this a sign of poor handling. The Ombudsman expects banks to engage with the details of your complaint, not avoid them.

The Ombudsman also reviews whether the bank followed the correct payment or card scheme rules. Card schemes have strict requirements for authorisation, declining transactions, handling disputes, and processing refunds. Direct debit rules are even stricter. If the bank misapplies scheme rules, the Ombudsman treats this as serious. Scheme rules protect customers. When banks ignore them or misunderstand them, the Ombudsman often finds in favour of the customer. The Ombudsman checks whether the bank followed these rules correctly.

Timeliness plays a significant role in the Ombudsman's assessment. If the bank delayed its investigation or provided late updates without reason, this reflects poor service. Timeliness matters because delays can worsen the impact. For example, a delayed refund may lead to charges from other companies. A delayed explanation may cause stress. The Ombudsman considers delays when deciding whether the bank treated the customer fairly. Timeliness is part of the duty to provide fair and efficient service.

The Ombudsman also checks whether the bank's final response included all mandatory information. Final responses must explain whether the complaint is upheld or not. They must explain the reasons for the decision. They must tell you about your right to escalate. If the final response lacks these elements, it may not meet FCA standards. Incomplete final responses weaken the bank's position. They show that the bank may not have taken the process seriously.

Another aspect the Ombudsman considers is whether the bank engaged with the complaint constructively. Constructive engagement means acknowledging errors when they occur, explaining decisions clearly, and taking steps to put things right. If the bank simply denies everything without evidence, the Ombudsman does not view this favourably. They expect banks to approach complaints professionally. Defensive or dismissive responses often signal poor handling. When the Ombudsman sees this behaviour, it can affect the final outcome.

The Ombudsman also pays attention to the language used in the bank's response. The tone matters. If the bank uses vague or generic statements, the Ombudsman questions whether the investigation was personalised. If the bank avoids addressing your points directly, the Ombudsman views this as incomplete handling. The Ombudsman expects banks to respond directly and clearly. Vague language weakens the credibility of the bank's position.

The Ombudsman's decision is based on evidence, not emotion. They focus on the facts, the timeline, the records, and the fairness of the outcome. They do not rely on rigid legal interpretation. They do not require customers to prove everything with absolute certainty. They take a balanced approach. If they believe that something is more likely than not, they can decide on that basis. This standard gives customers a fair chance, especially when some evidence is held only by the bank.

Once the Ombudsman completes their review, they form an initial view. This is not yet the final decision. It is the investigator's informal view of the case. The initial view explains what the Ombudsman believes is fair based on the evidence. It may support the bank, or it may support the customer. Many cases settle at this stage. If both sides accept the initial view, the case ends. If either side disagrees, the case can move to an Ombudsman for a final decision.

The Ombudsman's final decision is a detailed document. It explains the reasoning clearly. It explains the evidence considered. It explains the rules applied. It explains the fairness test. If you accept the final decision, it becomes binding on the bank. If you do not accept it, you are not bound by it, and you can choose other routes if available, such as court action. The Ombudsman's role is to give a fair and independent view. Their decisions are respected across the financial sector.

Understanding what the Ombudsman looks for helps you prepare strong submissions and clear summaries. It helps you focus on the evidence that matters. It helps you avoid unnecessary detail. It helps you understand how the Ombudsman will review the bank's reasoning. This knowledge strengthens your position and helps you approach the escalation process with confidence and a clear structure.

Chapter 9
How to Understand the Ombudsman's Initial View

When you receive the Ombudsman's initial view, you are looking at the first independent assessment of your complaint. This document is not a final decision, but it carries significant influence because it reflects the investigator's professional view of what happened, how the evidence fits together, and what outcome appears fair. Most complaints end at this stage because either the customer accepts the recommendation or the bank accepts it. Understanding how to read the initial view helps you decide whether it is fair, whether it reflects the evidence, and whether you should accept it or challenge it.

The initial view begins with a short explanation of the complaint. This summary tells you what the investigator, also referred to as an Adjudicator, believes the issue is about. It must match your original complaint. It must reflect the timeline you provided. It must include the key events. It must acknowledge the impact you raised. Read this section carefully. If the summary is wrong, the rest of the assessment may be affected. A misunderstanding at the start can make the entire review unreliable. If the summary is correct, the rest of the document is more likely to reflect the facts accurately.

The next part of the initial view explains what evidence the investigator reviewed. This is an important section because it shows what shaped their understanding. The investigator, may mention call recordings, transaction logs, security events, email communication, chat logs, branch interactions, or written correspondence. They may explain whether the bank provided complete evidence or whether something was missing. If the investigator does not mention important evidence, such as a call recording that you highlighted, this may indicate that they did not review it. The Ombudsman relies on a full and balanced review, so missing evidence matters. When reading this section, compare it to the evidence you provided and the evidence you expected the bank to provide.

The investigator then explains how they interpret the evidence. They may refer to the wording used during a call. They may refer to the exact time a payment was attempted. They may refer to the reason a card transaction was declined. They may refer to the messages exchanged with customer service. This interpretation section gives you insight into how the investigator sees the facts. If the interpretation matches the evidence, you can trust their reasoning more easily. If it does not match, you should note this for later consideration.

After explaining the facts, the investigator assesses whether the bank followed the correct rules. The Financial Ombudsman Service expects banks to follow the Financial Conduct Authority's principles, rules, and guidance. These include treating customers fairly, providing accurate information, using clear communication, handling complaints within eight weeks, and investigating complaints properly. The investigator also checks whether the bank followed industry rules such as the Direct Debit Guarantee or card scheme requirements. If the bank did not follow the correct rules, the investigator usually explains this clearly. If the bank did follow the rules, the investigator explains why the bank's actions were reasonable.

The initial view also addresses the impact of the issue. Impact matters because it helps determine what is fair. The investigator checks whether the impact you described was caused by the bank's actions, whether it was foreseeable, and whether the bank considered it properly. They check whether the impact resulted in financial loss, inconvenience, or stress. They then assess whether this impact influences the outcome. If the investigator ignores the impact, the assessment may be incomplete. The Ombudsman expects banks to take the practical and emotional consequences of mistakes seriously.

Another important part of the initial view is the investigator's reasoning. This section explains how they reached their conclusion. A strong assessment contains clear and logical reasoning. You should be able to follow each step. You should be able to see how the evidence relates to the conclusion. You should be able to understand why the investigator agrees or disagrees with the bank. If the reasoning is unclear, vague, or contradictory, this may indicate that the assessment is incomplete. Reasoning is one of the most important parts of the initial view because it shows how the investigator applied the fairness test.

The fairness test is central to the Ombudsman's work. Unlike courts, the Ombudsman does not rely strictly on legal standards. They ask what is fair and reasonable in the circumstances. They look at what happened, what should have happened, and what outcome is appropriate. Fairness involves both technical compliance and the practical reality of the situation. Fairness includes the impact. Fairness includes how the bank communicated. Fairness includes how the bank responded when things went wrong. The initial view must reflect this balance. If it does not, you may have grounds to ask for further review.

Another part of the initial view that requires attention is the conclusion about responsibility. The investigator explains whether they believe the bank caused the issue, contributed to it, or acted correctly. They explain whether you contributed to the problem. They explain whether circumstances outside your control played a role. They explain whether the evidence demonstrates that the bank's handling fell below the required standard. This conclusion is important because it forms the basis for any recommended redress.

The initial view also explains what the investigator believes should happen next. This may include a refund of charges, compensation, corrections to the account, removal of markers, or an apology. The investigator may also recommend that the bank sends clearer communication, changes internal records, or improves processes. These recommendations are based on the investigator's assessment of what is fair and reasonable. They represent the Ombudsman's position at this stage.

You should also check whether the initial view explains the limits of the investigation. The Ombudsman can only make decisions based on the evidence available. If evidence was missing, the investigator may mention this. Missing evidence does not automatically weaken your case, but it means the Ombudsman had to rely on what they had. Understanding the limits of the investigation helps you decide whether the initial view is fair.

After reading the initial view, your next task is to assess whether you agree with it. This does not require emotion. It requires calm and careful thought. Ask yourself whether the investigator understood your complaint. Ask yourself whether they reviewed the correct evidence. Ask yourself whether the reasoning makes sense. Ask yourself whether the outcome feels fair in light of the impact. If the assessment appears balanced and logical, accepting it may give you closure. If something is missing or inaccurate, you may decide to challenge it.

Understanding the initial view helps you make a thoughtful decision. It gives you insight into the Ombudsman's thinking. It shows you how they apply fairness. It shows you how they review evidence. It gives you a clear structure for deciding whether to accept or challenge the outcome.

Once you have read the opening sections of the initial view, the next step is to study how the investigator has broken down the events. The sequence of events is important because the Ombudsman bases much of its reasoning on what happened first, what followed next, and how the bank responded at each point. Many disputes arise not only from the main event, but from the way the bank handled the situation afterwards. When the investigator sets out the timeline, check whether the dates match your records. Check whether the order is correct. Check whether any key events are missing. Accurate timelines help ensure the fairness of the assessment. Incorrect timelines can affect the outcome.

The investigator then explains how the bank responded throughout the issue. This includes the quality of the advice, the clarity of communication, the accuracy of information, and the timeliness of updates. The Ombudsman expects banks to provide clear and correct information at all stages. If the bank gave unclear or incorrect advice, the investigator should comment on this. If the bank delayed in providing information, the investigator should acknowledge the delay. If the bank failed to explain what was happening, this should also appear in the assessment. This part of the initial view shows how deeply the investigator examined the bank's conduct and whether they took your communication concerns seriously.

Another part of the initial view discusses whether the bank's actions were reasonable in the circumstances. The term "reasonable" is central to the Ombudsman's approach. Reasonable actions depend not only on the rules, but on what an ordinary and fair-minded person would expect a bank to do in that situation. The investigator checks whether the bank should have taken extra steps. The investigator checks whether the bank overlooked information. The investigator checks whether the bank treated your circumstances with appropriate care. Understanding how the investigator views reasonableness helps you understand why they reached their conclusion and whether you agree with it.

The initial view also considers the bank's internal processes. Banks are required to follow their own procedures. These procedures exist to ensure consistency and fairness. If the bank failed to follow its own process, the investigator may highlight this as a service failure. For example, if the bank should have escalated the issue to a specialist team but did not, this may affect the fairness of the outcome. If the bank should have reviewed specific logs but failed to do so, this may weaken the bank's explanation. Process failures are important because they can indicate that the investigation was incomplete.

The Ombudsman also examines whether the bank's actions met the standards set out in the Financial Conduct Authority's rules. These rules require banks to act with integrity, treat customers fairly, communicate clearly, and handle complaints properly. The investigator checks whether the bank met these standards. They check whether the bank's actions matched the expectations of a regulated financial firm. If the investigator believes the bank failed to meet these standards, they explain why. This explanation shows how the Ombudsman applies the regulatory framework to real situations.

Another part of the initial view addresses how the bank documented the issue. Documentation includes call notes, account records, secure messages, and internal logs. The Ombudsman treats documentation as evidence. If the documentation does not reflect what actually happened, the investigator may question its reliability. For example, if a call recording contradicts the call notes, the investigator relies on the recording. If internal notes are vague or incomplete, the investigator may need to request further evidence. Documentation must be accurate for the bank's explanation to be accepted.

You should also examine how the investigator handled conflicting evidence. Conflicts arise when your evidence shows one account of events and the bank's evidence shows another. The investigator assesses which version is more likely. They rely on the standard of what is probably true based on the available evidence. This does not require absolute proof. It requires a balanced and fair judgment. When conflicting evidence is addressed in the initial view, check whether the investigator explained why one version was accepted over the other. Clear explanation is important for fairness.

Another section of the initial view deals with causation. Here, the investigator explains whether the bank's actions caused the problem or whether the issue resulted from something outside the bank's control. Causation is important because it influences the recommended outcome. If the bank caused the problem, the investigator may recommend redress. If something else caused the problem, the recommendation may be different. Understanding how the investigator views the cause helps you decide whether the conclusion is fair.

You should also look at how the investigator discusses the impact. Impact includes financial loss, practical inconvenience, stress, disruption, and time spent dealing with the problem. The investigator should explain how they assessed the impact. They should explain whether they believe the impact was significant. They should explain whether the bank addressed the impact in the final response. If the impact section is brief or incomplete, you may need to consider whether the assessment fully reflects the seriousness of the issue.

Another part of the initial view sets out the investigator's recommendation. This recommendation is based on the investigator's analysis of what is fair and reasonable. The recommendation may include financial redress, correction of records, reversal of charges, removal of markers, or changes to the account. It may also include an apology or improvements in communication. The investigator explains why they believe this outcome is appropriate. Compare this explanation with the reasoning. The recommendation should reflect the fairness test.

After reading the recommendation, you must consider whether it addresses the full scope of your complaint. The recommendation should cover each issue you raised. If you raised concerns about advice, payment problems, communication failures, and impact, the recommendation should address all of these. If the recommendation only covers part of the issue, the initial view may be incomplete. You should review whether the investigator overlooked anything important.

Another part of the initial view may address the bank's position. If the bank accepted responsibility during the investigation, the initial view reflects this. If the bank denied responsibility, the initial view explains whether the investigator agreed with the bank. The investigator may also comment on how the bank communicated during the complaint. If the bank provided unclear explanations or incomplete responses, the investigator may note this. These comments help you understand how the investigator assessed the bank's conduct throughout the process.

The initial view may also include comments about service quality. Service quality relates to delays, unclear communication, mistakes in handling the complaint, or failure to follow internal processes. Service quality issues may not always change the main outcome, but they affect fairness. If the bank's service was below the required standard, the investigator may recommend compensation for inconvenience. This reflects the principle that poor service should be acknowledged even if it did not directly cause financial loss.

The next step is deciding whether the initial view is fair. This requires calm and careful thought. You should first check whether the investigator understood the complaint. You should then assess whether the evidence they reviewed was complete. You should check whether the reasoning was clear. You should check whether the conclusion followed from the reasoning. You should check whether the recommended outcome reflects the impact and the seriousness of the issue. If everything is consistent, you may decide that the initial view is fair.

If you believe the initial view is not fair, you must identify why. You may believe the investigator misunderstood an important point. You may believe they did not review a key piece of evidence. You may believe they accepted the bank's explanation too easily. You may believe the recommended redress does not reflect the impact. You may believe the timeline was read incorrectly. You may believe the investigator did not comment on relevant rules. If something is missing or inaccurate, you can challenge the initial view. Challenges must be factual, structured, and supported by evidence.

Understanding the initial view gives you control. It helps you make an informed decision about whether to accept the recommendation or ask for further review. It shows you how the Ombudsman assessed the evidence. It shows you how they applied fairness. It shows you whether the bank's actions were considered properly. When you understand the structure and purpose of the initial view, you can respond with confidence and clarity.

Chapter 10
How to Challenge the Ombudsman's Initial View

Challenging the Ombudsman's initial view is one of the most important decisions you will make in your complaint journey. The initial view is the investigator's early assessment of what happened, what the evidence shows, and what outcome appears fair. It is not a final decision, but it carries considerable weight because most complaints end at this stage. Many people accept the initial view, either because it is fair or because they feel they have no grounds to dispute it. Others challenge the view because they believe the investigator misunderstood the issue, missed key evidence, or applied the rules incorrectly. A challenge can strengthen your position, but only when it is clear, structured, and based on evidence.

Before preparing a challenge, you must read the initial view carefully and without rushing. The first thing to look for is how the investigator summarised your complaint. This summary must reflect your original submission. It must include the correct timeline, the correct description of events, and the correct explanation of the impact. If the summary is inaccurate, the rest of the assessment may also be affected. Errors in this section can indicate misunderstandings that influence the reasoning and the final outcome. If the summary is correct, the investigation has a stronger foundation.

The next part of the initial view explains what evidence the investigator reviewed. Evidence is the foundation of fairness, so this section must match what you expect. The investigator may refer to call recordings, transaction logs, internal notes, security events, email communication, or written correspondence. They may describe what they found in each record. If you notice that a key piece of evidence is missing from this list, you should note it immediately. Missing evidence is a common and valid ground for challenging the initial view. For example, if the issue involved incorrect advice and the investigator did not mention listening to the relevant call recording, this is an important omission.

After describing the evidence, the investigator explains their interpretation of it. Interpretation is important because it influences the reasoning and the conclusion. The investigator may describe what a call adviser said, how a payment was processed, or why a transaction was declined. They may describe the sequence of messages or the details of a complaint response. If the interpretation does not match your understanding or the content of the evidence, you must examine this section closely. Interpretation errors are serious because they can lead to incorrect conclusions.

The initial view then considers whether the bank followed the correct rules. The Financial Conduct Authority's rules, principles, and guidance set standards for how banks must behave. These standards cover clarity, fairness, accuracy, competence, and proper complaint handling. The investigator explains whether the bank met these standards. They may comment on whether the bank gave correct information, whether they acted within reasonable timeframes, or whether they investigated the complaint properly. They may also comment on industry rules such as card scheme requirements or direct debit rules. If the investigator's assessment of rule compliance is unclear or incomplete, this may be a point for challenge.

The initial view also discusses the impact of the issue. Impact is important because it shows how the problem affected your daily life. It may include financial loss, inconvenience, practical disruption, or stress. The investigator should explain whether they believe the impact was caused by the bank's actions, whether it was significant, and whether the bank addressed it. If the initial view does not consider impact properly, the assessment may not reflect the seriousness of the issue. This is a common reason for challenges.

Another important part of the initial view is the reasoning. The investigator's reasoning explains how they reached their conclusion. It shows how they weighed the evidence, how they interpreted the timeline, and how they applied the fairness test. You should examine the reasoning carefully. It must be logical and consistent. If the investigator makes a statement that does not follow from the evidence, this is a valid point for challenge. If the reasoning relies on assumptions rather than facts, this must be highlighted. Reasoning is central to fairness, so errors in this section are significant.

The reasoning leads to the conclusion. The conclusion summarises whether the bank acted fairly, whether the bank's actions caused the problem, and what the investigator believes is a fair outcome. The conclusion should be brief but clear. If you believe the conclusion does not reflect the reasoning or the evidence, you must note this. Conclusions must match the facts presented earlier in the document. If they do not, the initial view may be flawed.

After the conclusion, the investigator explains what they believe the bank should do next. This may include correcting records, refunding money, compensating for inconvenience, removing markers, or improving communication. You should check whether these steps address the full scope of your complaint. If the recommended action is incomplete, you may need to challenge the view. For example, if the investigator recommends a refund but ignores the wider impact, the outcome may not be fair.

Before deciding whether to challenge the initial view, you must examine whether the investigator understood your circumstances. Circumstances matter because they influence the fairness test. For example, if you were in financial difficulty and the bank ignored this, the consequences may be more serious. If the investigator did not consider your circumstances, this may weaken the assessment. You must check whether the initial view acknowledges any factors you raised.

You should also consider the tone of the initial view. The tone should be calm, neutral, and factual. It should not feel dismissive. It should not feel rushed. It should reflect a careful review. While tone does not determine fairness, it can help you understand whether the investigator approached the case thoughtfully.

Once you have completed your review of the initial view, your next step is to decide whether to accept or challenge it. Accepting the view may be sensible if the assessment is fair, the reasoning is clear, and the outcome resolves the issue. Rejecting the view may be necessary if key evidence was missed, if the reasoning is flawed, or if the conclusion does not match the facts. This decision requires calm judgement.

If you believe the initial view is incorrect, you must prepare a structured challenge. Challenges cannot rely on emotion. They must rely on evidence, clarity, and logic. A strong challenge explains exactly what is wrong with the initial view and why it matters. It identifies specific issues, not general dissatisfaction. Each point must be supported by evidence.

Challenging the initial view is an important step in ensuring fairness. It protects your right to a full and accurate review. It ensures that mistakes do not shape the final decision. Understanding how to challenge effectively gives you confidence and structure as you move through the complaints process.

Once you have identified the specific issues you disagree with in the initial view, your next task is to shape your challenge in a way that is clear, structured, and easy for the investigator to follow. The Ombudsman takes challenges seriously. They expect your points to be factual and supported by evidence. A well-structured challenge helps the investigator understand exactly where the initial view may be incomplete or incorrect. This increases the chances of the view being revised before the case goes to a final decision.

A clear challenge begins with a short introduction. This introduction simply states that you have reviewed the initial view and that you have identified points that require clarification or correction. You do not need to explain your feelings about the view. You do not need to describe your frustration or disappointment. The Ombudsman responds best to factual summaries that show calm understanding. A brief introduction sets the tone and signals that your challenge is organised and reasonable.

The next step is to set out your points one by one. Each point should focus on a specific issue in the initial view. Begin each point with a short heading that explains the topic. The heading should reflect the exact problem, such as missing evidence, incorrect interpretation, errors in the timeline, overlooked circumstances, or incomplete assessment of impact. Headings help the investigator see the structure of your challenge. They also help the investigator identify which parts of the initial view you are referring to.

After the heading, you should explain your point clearly. Begin by describing what the initial view said. Then explain why you believe it is incorrect or incomplete. Use evidence to support your explanation. If the investigator missed a call recording, identify the recording and explain what it contains. If the investigator misinterpreted a screenshot, explain what the screenshot actually shows. If the investigator misunderstood the timeline, list the correct dates and explain the error. If the investigator accepted a bank explanation that does not match the logs, explain the difference. Every point must have a clear link to the evidence.

Evidence is central to any challenge. You must be precise when referring to evidence. If you mention a call recording, identify the date and the key detail. If you mention a screenshot, explain the specific information it contains. If you mention an email or a message, describe the relevant sentence. If the investigator misread the evidence, point out how and why. The Ombudsman relies on evidence, so the more accurately you refer to it, the stronger your challenge becomes.

Timelines are another area where challenges often succeed. If the investigator misunderstood the timing of events, this can affect the fairness of the assessment. For example, if the investigator believed a delay was short when it was long, the impact may be underestimated. If the investigator believed you reported the issue later than you did, they may have assumed the bank acted fairly when they did not. If you believe the timeline was read incorrectly, explain the correct sequence clearly. Provide the dates. Provide the times if relevant. Explain how the timeline affects the reasoning.

Another important part of a challenge is addressing the investigator's analysis of the bank's behaviour. If the investigator accepted the bank's notes without checking the underlying evidence, you must highlight this. Notes may not always reflect what actually happened. If the bank's explanation is contradicted by recordings or logs, explain this clearly. The Ombudsman expects investigators to check the most reliable evidence. If you believe the investigator relied on weaker evidence, this is a strong point for challenge.

Circumstances matter when assessing fairness. If the investigator did not consider your circumstances, or if they misunderstood them, this can affect the outcome. Circumstances include health issues, financial difficulty, communication needs, or major life events. If your circumstances were relevant and the investigator did not address them, explain this. You should not exaggerate or dramatise your situation. You should explain calmly why your circumstances increased the seriousness of the impact and why they should have been considered.

Another part of your challenge should address the impact assessment. If the investigator overlooked the impact or underestimated it, you must explain why this affects fairness. Impact includes the practical consequences of the issue, the stress caused, the time spent resolving it, and any financial loss. If the initial view fails to recognise how disruptive the issue was, explain the details clearly. Provide specific examples. Do not use emotional language. Do not make general statements. Describe what happened and how it affected your daily life.

You should also address the recommended outcome. If the initial view includes recommendations that do not address the full scope of your complaint, explain this. For example, if the investigator recommended a refund but did not recommend correcting a marker on your account, this may not resolve the issue. If the investigator recommended compensation but ignored the need for records to be corrected, the outcome may be incomplete. Explain why the recommended outcome does not address all aspects of the problem. Provide evidence or reasoning to support your view.

When writing your challenge, avoid repeating your original complaint. The Ombudsman has already read it. A challenge is not a second opportunity to explain everything from the beginning. It is a targeted response to the initial view. You must focus on the specific issues that affect the fairness of the assessment. Repeating your original points without linking them to the initial view will not strengthen your case. Structure and clarity matter more than volume.

Tone is important when challenging the initial view. The Ombudsman responds best to calm and factual writing. You should not show anger. You should not use emotional language. You should not accuse the investigator of wrongdoing. Instead, you should explain what you believe is incorrect and why. A calm and structured challenge shows the Ombudsman that you understand the process and that you are focused on fairness. This increases the chances that your challenge will be taken seriously and reviewed carefully.

After completing your challenge, read it again to ensure that each point is clear. Mistakes or unclear writing can weaken your position. Check that you have supported each point with evidence. Check that you have explained why each point matters. Check that the challenge is consistent and organised. Once you are satisfied, you can submit it. The investigator will review it and decide whether to amend the initial view. If they do not amend it, the case will be passed to an Ombudsman for a final decision.

When a challenge is well structured, it gives you the best chance of having the initial view revised. It shows the Ombudsman that you took time to review the evidence carefully. It helps them understand where the initial view may be incomplete or incorrect. It strengthens your position by focusing on facts, not emotion. The Ombudsman process is built on fairness. A clear and well-reasoned challenge ensures that fairness is applied to your case.

Chapter 11

What Happens When Your Case Is Referred to an Ombudsman for a Final Decision

When your case is referred to an Ombudsman for a final decision, the complaint moves into its most formal stage. Up to this point, your complaint has been handled by an investigator. The investigator reviewed the evidence, assessed the reasoning, prepared an initial view, and attempted to resolve the matter through an informal process. If you or the bank disagreed with that initial view, the complaint was unable to conclude at that stage. A final decision is required because a disagreement remains about what is fair and reasonable. This final step is important because it provides certainty. The Ombudsman's final decision is binding on the bank if you accept it. Understanding what happens at this stage helps you prepare and lowers uncertainty about the process.

Once the case is ready for a final decision, the Ombudsman reviews everything from the beginning. They do not rely only on the investigator's initial view. They complete their own independent assessment. They read your original complaint. They review your challenge to the initial view. They examine the bank's file. They examine the investigator's notes. They listen to recordings. They check messages. They read the correspondence. They review transaction and security logs. They take time to understand the full picture. The Ombudsman's role is to reach a fair and reasonable outcome based on all available evidence. This level of review ensures that the final decision reflects a complete and independent assessment.

The Ombudsman begins by reviewing the summary of the complaint. They confirm that the issue has been described accurately. They check the timeline. They check the specific points you raised. They check the core issue that led to disagreement. If the summary is incorrect, the Ombudsman may ask the investigator or the parties for clarification. This protects the fairness of the process. A correct understanding of the complaint is the foundation for a fair decision.

Next, the Ombudsman reviews the evidence. Evidence is central to the final decision. The Ombudsman may review call recordings again if they believe something requires further attention. They may request additional logs from the bank. They may ask the investigator to confirm which records were reviewed. The Ombudsman checks whether any evidence was overlooked in the initial view. They check whether any evidence was misinterpreted. They check whether the evidence supports the explanations given by both you and the bank. This step ensures that the final decision reflects the full facts rather than assumptions or partial information.

The Ombudsman then assesses whether the bank followed the correct rules. The Financial Conduct Authority's principles, rules, and guidance inform the Ombudsman's approach. These rules require banks to act fairly, communicate clearly, handle complaints properly, and provide accurate information. The Ombudsman checks whether these duties were met. They also consider industry rules, such as card scheme requirements and direct debit rules. If the bank failed to meet these standards, this will influence the final decision. If the bank followed the rules but still caused harm, the Ombudsman examines whether the outcome is still unfair in the circumstances.

The Ombudsman assesses the fairness of the bank's actions by examining both processes and outcomes. They check whether the bank responded appropriately when the issue was reported. They check whether the bank acted within reasonable timeframes. They check whether the bank investigated the issue properly. They check whether the bank's explanations are supported by the evidence. They check whether the bank considered your circumstances. They check whether the bank recognised the impact and took steps to resolve the problem. Fairness is not determined only by technical compliance. It includes the real effect on your life.

The Ombudsman also reviews your challenge to the initial view. They check whether the points you raised were addressed. They check whether the investigator overlooked evidence. They check whether the reasoning was incomplete. They check whether you highlighted relevant circumstances that were not considered. They check whether you provided evidence that changes the understanding of the case. They check whether your arguments influence the fairness test. The final decision reflects the Ombudsman's review of both the initial view and your response to it.

Another part of the review is examining the bank's response to the initial view. If the bank disagreed with the initial view, the Ombudsman reviews the bank's points as well. The Ombudsman expects the bank's disagreements to be factual and supported by evidence, just as they expect from you. If the bank agreed with the initial view but you did not, the Ombudsman reviews whether your challenge raises strong reasons to change the outcome. The Ombudsman considers both sides of the dispute with equal weight.

The Ombudsman then considers causation. This means determining whether the bank's actions caused the issue, contributed to it, or failed to prevent harm. Causation is important because it shapes the recommended outcome. If the bank caused the problem, the Ombudsman is likely to recommend corrective action and appropriate redress. If the bank did not cause the problem but handled it poorly, the Ombudsman may recommend different redress. Understanding causation helps the Ombudsman decide what is fair based on the evidence.

Impact is another key part of the assessment. The Ombudsman reviews how the issue affected you. They consider financial loss, practical inconvenience, disruption, and stress. They consider whether the bank should reasonably have foreseen the impact. They consider whether the bank's response made the impact worse. They consider whether the bank acknowledged the impact in their final response. Impact influences the level of redress. A final decision that ignores impact is incomplete, so the Ombudsman examines it carefully.

Once the Ombudsman has reviewed the evidence, the reasoning, the rules, the impact, and the challenges raised, they begin forming their decision. The final decision must be clear. It must explain the facts. It must explain what evidence was considered. It must explain how the fairness test was applied. It must explain how the rules were interpreted. It must explain why the outcome is appropriate. The Ombudsman writes the decision carefully, because it is binding on the bank if you accept it.

The final decision is not a negotiation. It is not an offer. It is a conclusion. If you accept the final decision, it becomes binding on the bank. The bank must follow it. They must provide the redress required. They must make corrections. They must apologise if instructed. They must carry out any other steps set out in the decision. If you accept, the case closes.

If you do not accept the final decision, the bank is not bound by it. You can choose not to accept it if you believe it is not fair. You may then consider other options, such as legal action. The final decision gives you clarity on what the Ombudsman believes is fair. Whether you accept it is your decision.

Once the Ombudsman forms their view of the facts, they begin writing the final decision. This document is formal, clear, and detailed. It differs from the initial view because it reflects the Ombudsman's independent judgement rather than the investigator's. The Ombudsman writes in a direct and precise style. They avoid unnecessary language. They focus on what matters. The structure of the decision helps you understand how they reached their conclusion and what the outcome means for you.

The final decision begins with a summary of the complaint. This summary sets out the issue in simple terms. It explains what you raised, how the bank responded, and why the case reached this stage. The Ombudsman restates the complaint to ensure that both parties have the same understanding. This avoids confusion and ensures clarity. The summary will often cover the key events and the main points of disagreement. It provides a clear starting point for the rest of the decision.

After the summary, the Ombudsman explains the evidence they reviewed. This may include call recordings, transaction logs, internal notes, security events, and correspondence. The Ombudsman states what they found in each piece of evidence. They explain how the evidence supports or contradicts the explanations given by both you and the bank. This section is important because it shows the depth of the review. It also shows how the Ombudsman interpreted the facts.

The Ombudsman then explains how they applied the rules. They consider the Financial Conduct Authority's principles, rules, and guidance. They consider whether the bank treated you fairly, communicated clearly, and handled the complaint properly. They consider whether the bank followed industry rules or internal processes. They consider whether the bank acted within reasonable timeframes. They explain how these rules affect the fairness test. This step ensures that the final decision reflects both the evidence and the regulatory expectations placed on the bank.

Next, the Ombudsman examines causation. They explain whether the bank caused the issue, contributed to it, or should have prevented it. They explain whether your actions played a role. They explain whether the problem was outside anyone's control. This section clarifies the relationship between the events and the outcome. It helps you understand why the Ombudsman believes the bank is or is not responsible for what happened.

Impact is also assessed in detail. The Ombudsman explains how the issue affected you. They consider financial loss, inconvenience, disruption, and stress. They consider whether the impact was foreseeable. They consider whether the bank should have taken steps to reduce the impact. They explain whether the impact justifies compensation or corrective action. The Ombudsman takes impact seriously because it reflects the real effect of the issue on your life.

After reviewing the evidence, the reasoning, the rules, causation, and impact, the Ombudsman sets out their conclusion. This conclusion is clear and direct. It states whether the bank acted fairly. It states whether the bank handled the issue properly. It states whether the bank must take action to put things right. The conclusion may support the initial view, or it may differ from it. The Ombudsman is not bound by the investigator's recommendation. They form their own independent judgement.

The final decision also includes instructions for the bank. If the complaint is upheld, the Ombudsman explains what the bank must do. This may include refunding charges, correcting records, reversing interest, removing markers, providing compensation, or issuing a written apology. The instructions are specific. They tell the bank exactly what steps are required. This ensures that the bank takes the correct action within the correct timeframe.

If the complaint is not upheld, the Ombudsman explains why. They explain which evidence supports the bank's position. They explain how the rules apply to the situation. They explain why the bank's actions were fair and reasonable. A detailed explanation helps you understand why the decision was made even if you disagree with it.

Once you receive the final decision, you must make a choice. If you accept the decision, it becomes binding on the bank. The bank must follow it. They must provide the redress. They must make the corrections. They must apologise if required. They must follow every instruction in the decision. Accepting the decision closes the case. It gives you certainty and allows you to move forward.

If you do not accept the final decision, the outcome is different. The decision does not become binding on the bank. The bank does not have to follow it. The Ombudsman's involvement ends. You may choose to take legal action or explore other options if you believe the decision is not fair. The Ombudsman does not enforce decisions you do not accept. They provide clarity, but the choice is yours.

Understanding the weight of the final decision is important. This document represents the highest level of independent assessment in the financial complaints process. It reflects a careful review of the evidence and the rules. It reflects clear reasoning. It reflects the fairness test. Accepting or rejecting the decision is a personal choice, but understanding the process helps you make an informed one.

After the Ombudsman issues the final decision, the bank must act within a reasonable timeframe. They may need to make changes to your account, issue refunds, or provide compensation. They may need to update records or correct information. They may need to send you confirmation once the actions have been completed. The Ombudsman expects banks to complete required actions promptly and without delay. If the bank fails to comply, you can contact the Ombudsman for support.

You should keep a copy of the final decision for your records. This document may be useful in the future, especially if you need to reference the findings or show that the bank accepted responsibility. The final decision provides a clear narrative of what happened and what the Ombudsman believed was fair. It is an important record that you should store securely.

The final decision stage is the last point in the Ombudsman process. Once accepted, there is no further right to appeal within the Ombudsman service. The decision provides closure. It provides certainty. It provides clarity. If you accept it, the case ends with a clear outcome and a clear explanation. If you reject it, you have the option to pursue other routes, but the Ombudsman's involvement ends.

Understanding what happens when your case is referred to an Ombudsman for a final decision helps you prepare for the outcome. It reduces uncertainty. It gives you confidence. It shows you how the process works and what to expect. It helps you make informed decisions at each step. When you understand the process, you are in a stronger position to protect your rights and ensure fairness.

Chapter 12

How to Take Your Complaint Further After the Final Decision

When the Ombudsman issues a final decision, it marks the highest point of the financial complaints process. This decision reflects a complete and independent review of the facts, the rules, the communication, and the evidence. It represents the Ombudsman's formal view of what is fair and reasonable. Once you receive the final decision, the complaint has reached a natural conclusion within the Ombudsman service. At this stage, you must decide how to proceed. You can accept the decision, reject it, or consider other routes if the outcome does not resolve the issue. Understanding these options helps you make an informed and confident choice.

If you accept the final decision, the case ends. The bank becomes legally bound to follow the outcome. They must carry out every instruction in the decision. This may include refunding money, correcting records, providing compensation, or issuing a written apology. The bank cannot negotiate, delay without reason, or offer an alternative outcome. They must follow the instructions exactly. Accepting the decision gives you certainty and closure. It brings the dispute to an end with a clear outcome supported by a transparent review.

If you choose not to accept the final decision, the outcome is different. The decision does not become binding on the bank. They are not required to follow it. The Ombudsman cannot enforce it. The Ombudsman's involvement ends once you decline the decision. Declining does not mean the process was wasted. The final decision still provides a detailed record of what happened and the Ombudsman's view of the facts. This record can help you decide what to do next. Declining the decision simply means you wish to explore other routes outside the Ombudsman process.

Before deciding whether to take your complaint further, you must understand the purpose of the Ombudsman. The Ombudsman is designed to resolve disputes through fairness and evidence. It is an alternative to the courts. It is intended to be simpler, faster, and less stressful than litigation. Once the Ombudsman has reviewed your case and issued a final decision, you have received the most complete independent assessment available outside a courtroom. If the outcome does not resolve the issue, you must consider whether a separate route is suitable for your situation.

One route available after rejecting the final decision is legal action. Legal action involves taking the dispute to court. Courts follow formal legal procedures and strict rules of evidence. They do not use the fairness test used by the Ombudsman. They rely on case law, statutory law, and legal interpretation. Legal action can be complex and costly. It may require legal advice. It may require representation. Before considering legal action, you must weigh the risks and potential costs. The court may reach a different conclusion, but the process is longer and more demanding than the Ombudsman route.

Before taking legal action, you may need to follow a pre action protocol. Pre action protocols require parties to exchange information and attempt to resolve the dispute before issuing court proceedings. You must follow the correct protocol for your type of case. Failure to follow the protocol can lead to cost consequences. The protocol requires clear communication, factual summaries, and attempts to resolve the matter without court involvement. If you choose the legal route, you must ensure that you understand the protocol and follow it properly.

Legal advice can help you decide whether court action is appropriate. A solicitor can explain the legal strength of your case, the potential cost, and the likelihood of success. They can provide guidance on the best route forward. They can explain whether the evidence supports a legal claim. They can explain whether the court is likely to accept your argument. Not every dispute is suitable for court action, so legal advice helps you make an informed decision. If you cannot afford a solicitor, you may consider free legal advice services or consumer rights organisations that provide guidance.

Another route to consider is alternative dispute resolution outside the Ombudsman service. Some organisations offer mediation or negotiation services. Mediation can help both parties reach an agreement without formal court action. Mediation is less adversarial and can provide flexible outcomes. It may also be cheaper and faster than litigation. Whether mediation is suitable depends on the nature of the dispute and whether both parties are willing to participate. Mediation requires cooperation. It cannot proceed if one party refuses.

You may also consider regulatory escalation. The Financial Conduct Authority does not resolve individual disputes. They do not intervene in personal complaints. However, they use complaint information to monitor banks and identify patterns of misconduct. If you believe that your issue indicates a wider problem affecting other customers, you may report the matter to the regulator. This does not resolve your personal case, but it contributes to regulatory oversight and may influence how banks behave in the future.

Taking your complaint further after the final decision also requires understanding the limitation period for legal action. Legal claims must be brought within specific time limits. These limits vary depending on the nature of the claim. For example, claims relating to contract disputes generally have longer limitation periods than claims relating to negligence. If you are considering court action, you must check the relevant limitation period. Courts cannot hear claims submitted after the deadline unless certain exceptional circumstances apply.

You should also consider whether further action will produce a meaningful outcome. The Ombudsman process is designed to be accessible and fair. It provides detailed reasoning and clear outcomes. If the Ombudsman has rejected your complaint or upheld only part of it, you must assess whether court action would produce a different result. Courts rely on legal standards, not the fairness test. The Ombudsman may consider factors that courts cannot. This means that in some cases, the Ombudsman may provide a more favourable assessment than a court. Understanding these differences helps you decide the best route for your situation.

Another point to consider is the emotional and practical cost of further action. Legal disputes require time, effort, and organisation. They can be stressful. They may require documents, statements, and preparation. If the value of the dispute is low, further action may not be proportionate. If the value is high, legal action may be more appropriate. You must assess whether you are willing and able to continue the process. This decision requires clear thinking and honest reflection.

If you choose not to take further action, the Ombudsman's final decision still provides closure. Even if you do not accept it formally, it gives you insight into what happened, what could have been done differently, and how the rules were applied. It provides clarity, which can help you move forward. The decision is independent and detailed. It offers perspective on the dispute and can guide your future decisions as a consumer.

Understanding how to take your complaint further after the final decision is about knowing your options and understanding the implications of each route. It helps you make a calm and informed choice. It ensures that you do not feel pressured or uncertain. It gives you a clear structure for deciding whether to accept the outcome, reject it, or pursue another path. Decision making after the final decision requires clarity, patience, and careful thought.

Once you understand the routes available after a final decision, the next step is to evaluate each option with a clear and realistic mindset. The financial complaints framework is designed to give people a fair and accessible pathway for resolving disputes. The Ombudsman's final decision plays a central role in that process. Even so, there are circumstances where you may feel the issue remains unresolved, the reasoning does not address your concerns, or the outcome does not reflect the impact. In these situations, making the right choice about the next step is important.

If you choose to reject the final decision, you must understand that you are stepping outside the Ombudsman's jurisdiction. The rights and protections you have within the Ombudsman process no longer apply. When you reject a final decision, the complaint does not return for further review. It does not move to another level within the Ombudsman service. The Ombudsman cannot reconsider the case or alter the decision. Rejecting the decision simply means you are choosing to explore external routes. This shift in responsibility is important because you take full control of how the dispute progresses from this point forward.

Before taking action outside the Ombudsman, you should consider the strength of your case from a legal perspective. The fairness test used by the Ombudsman is broader than the legal tests used by courts. The Ombudsman can consider circumstances, communication failures, poor service, and the general reasonableness of the bank's actions. Courts cannot. Courts rely on strict legal rules. This difference means that some cases that succeed before the Ombudsman may not succeed in a court. You should consider whether your dispute relies on fairness or legal entitlement. This distinction helps you assess whether further action is realistic.

If you believe you have a strong legal case, the next step is to consider the practical implications of court action. Court action involves formal procedures. You must submit a claim, pay fees, prepare evidence, and follow strict timelines. The bank will almost certainly defend the claim and may use solicitors. You may also need legal representation, especially if the value of the claim is significant or if the issues are complex. Courts expect parties to comply with procedural rules. Mistakes can lead to delays, increased costs, or even dismissal of the claim. You must be prepared for a structured and demanding process.

If you decide to pursue legal action, you should gather the documents you submitted to the Ombudsman. These documents provide a clear framework for your case. They contain the timeline, the evidence, the communication history, and the impact. They also contain the Ombudsman's findings, which outline how an independent body viewed the dispute. Courts will not be bound by the Ombudsman's decision, but the decision may help structure your arguments. The Ombudsman's findings can provide clarity, even if you do not accept them. They can highlight weaknesses, strengths, and gaps in the evidence that are relevant to legal action.

If you are not ready to go to court, you may consider informal negotiation with the bank. Some banks will negotiate after the Ombudsman process ends if they believe it is in their interest to resolve the dispute. This depends on the bank, the evidence, and the circumstances. Negotiation gives you flexibility and avoids the cost and formality of legal action. You can present the Ombudsman's findings to support your position. You can propose a settlement that reflects the impact. You can explain why the final decision did not address the issue in a way you believe is fair. Negotiation does not guarantee success, but it can lead to practical outcomes without the stress of litigation.

Another option is to escalate your concerns to consumer protection bodies or advocacy organisations. These groups cannot overturn the Ombudsman's decision or intervene in your personal dispute. However, they can provide guidance, help you understand your rights, and suggest possible routes for further action. They may also be aware of wider issues affecting customers at the same bank. If your experience reflects a pattern of poor service or misconduct, reporting the issue can help these organisations raise concerns with regulators. This does not resolve your case, but it contributes to wider protection for consumers.

If you believe the bank's conduct raises regulatory concerns, you may also report the matter to the Financial Conduct Authority. The regulator cannot investigate your individual complaint, but they accept information about potential breaches of rules. Your report may contribute to a broader regulatory review or investigation. This route does not change your personal outcome, but it plays a role in consumer protection and regulatory oversight. The FCA treats reports confidentially and uses them to identify patterns or systemic issues within the financial sector.

If you choose not to take further action, you should still reflect on what the process has taught you. The Ombudsman's final decision provides a clear record of the facts, the evidence, and the reasoning. It may highlight areas where communication could have been clearer, where actions could have been more careful, or where expectations may have been different. These insights can help you in future dealings with financial firms. They can help you recognise warning signs, ask better questions, and protect yourself from similar issues in the future.

One practical step after the final decision is to review your financial arrangements. If the dispute revealed weaknesses in the bank's processes or communication, you may consider whether you want to remain with the bank. Consumer choice allows you to move to a bank that provides clearer communication, stronger support, or better service. Changing banks is a practical step that can improve your confidence and protect your future financial stability. The final decision provides information that helps you decide whether staying with the bank is the best choice.

Another step is to organise your documents for long term reference. Even if you accept the Ombudsman's decision, you may need to refer to the case in the future. Banks must act in line with the decision, and having a complete record helps you confirm whether they have followed the instructions. Keeping the documents clear and accessible also helps if any related issues arise later. Good record keeping protects your rights and ensures you have the information you need if the matter ever resurfaces.

If you feel unsure after reading the final decision, you may choose to take time before deciding. The Ombudsman gives you a deadline to accept or decline the decision, but you do not need to decide immediately. Taking time to read the decision again can give you clarity. You may also find it helpful to discuss the decision with someone you trust. Talking through the reasoning and impact can help you understand whether the outcome reflects your expectations of fairness. This time also allows you to consider the practical implications of taking further action.

Taking your complaint further after the final decision requires clear thinking. You must balance fairness, practicality, cost, time, and emotional impact. You must understand what each option involves. You must understand the consequences of accepting or rejecting the decision. You must consider the strength of your case and your ability to pursue it. These decisions require calm reflection and careful judgement.

Understanding your options after the final decision ensures that you remain in control of your complaint journey. It gives you clarity. It gives you structure. It gives you confidence. Whether you accept the outcome or pursue another route, you are making an informed choice. This chapter helps you understand how the final stage fits into the wider complaints process and what steps are available if the issue remains unresolved.

Conclusion

Bringing Your Complaint Journey Together

Reaching the conclusion of this guide brings the entire complaints process into a clear and organised structure. By this point, you have learned how banks handle complaints, what rules they must follow, what rights you have at every stage, and how to move your complaint forward with confidence. This final chapter brings together the key principles, methods, and expectations that you have explored. It also explains how you can use what you have learned to protect yourself in future dealings with financial firms.

Your journey began with understanding the structure of the complaints system. Banks follow a single stage complaints process, followed by the Financial Ombudsman Service. This structure is simple on the surface, yet many people struggle with it because they do not know what banks must do, how quickly they must respond, or how to improve the strength of their complaint before escalation. You learned that banks have a regulatory duty to investigate complaints fairly, provide clear information, and issue a final response within specific timelines. This knowledge keeps you in control. It prevents the bank from leading the process on its own terms. It gives you the foundation to challenge delays, vague responses, or poor investigations.

You also learned the importance of setting out your complaint clearly. Many people submit complaints in an emotional or unfocused way. This weakens their position. You learned that clarity is the strongest tool you have. When you explain what happened, when it happened, why it matters, and what you want done, you give the bank a complete structure to follow. You reduce the chances of misunderstanding. You guide the investigation. You help the bank understand the facts quickly. A clear complaint is not only easier for the bank to assess, it also becomes stronger evidence if the matter later goes to the Ombudsman.

Understanding your rights was another important part of your learning. You learned that banks must follow strict rules set by the Financial Conduct Authority. These rules guide everything the bank does, from communication to complaint handling. You learned that you have the right to a fair review, the right to clear explanations, the right to evidence based outcomes, and the right to escalate if the bank fails to resolve the matter. These rights exist to protect you from poor service and unfair decisions. Knowing them makes you more confident and more capable during the complaints process.

One of the most important lessons you learned is how to challenge a weak or incomplete complaint response. Banks do not always investigate fully. They may overlook evidence. They may misinterpret events. They may issue generic responses that do not explain the reasoning. You learned how to recognise weak responses and how to challenge them using structure, clarity, and evidence. This turns a poor complaint response into an opportunity to strengthen your case. The skill of challenging a weak response helps you not only in this complaint, but in every future complaint you make.

You also learned how to prepare your case for the Financial Ombudsman Service. Many people escalate too early or without preparing properly. You learned that preparation involves organising your evidence, clarifying the timeline, identifying the gaps in the bank's response, and presenting your case in a structured and factual way. The Ombudsman works with evidence and reasoning, not emotion or frustration. Knowing this helps you write submissions that are easy to follow and hard to dismiss. It helps you stand out as someone who understands the process and respects the structure of the review.

Another central lesson was understanding how the Ombudsman thinks. The Ombudsman uses the fairness test. They look at the rules, the evidence, the impact, the timeline, and the circumstances. They are not on the bank's side and they are not on your side. They focus entirely on whether the bank acted in a fair and reasonable way. You learned what evidence matters most to the Ombudsman and how to present it clearly. You learned how the Ombudsman treats missing evidence, incorrect assumptions, and poor reasoning. This knowledge allows you to shape your submissions so they match the Ombudsman's approach.

Understanding the Ombudsman's initial view was another important lesson. Many people feel anxious when they receive the initial view. They do not know how much weight it carries or what to do if they disagree with it. You learned that the initial view is not final. It is a starting point for resolution. You learned how to read it carefully, identify errors, understand the reasoning, and challenge it effectively. The ability to challenge an initial view is one of the strongest skills you can take from this book. It gives you confidence and clarity when faced with an early assessment you believe is incomplete.

You also learned that the Ombudsman's final decision is the last step in the process. You learned how it is written, what it includes, and how it becomes binding if you accept it. You learned the difference between accepting and rejecting the decision, and the consequences of each choice. This knowledge prepares you for the final stage and helps you make decisions based on clarity rather than uncertainty.

The final chapters taught you what to do if the issue remains unresolved after the final decision. You learned how to weigh the risks of legal action, how to prepare for alternative dispute routes, and how to consider the practical and emotional cost of further steps. You learned that taking a complaint further after the final decision requires careful judgement, not pressure or frustration. The final chapters give you the structure needed to think clearly about the options available outside the Ombudsman process.

This conclusion builds on all of these lessons. It gives you a full understanding of how the complaints process works, how to navigate it confidently, and how to protect your rights at every stage. Knowing this process strengthens you as a consumer and prepares you for any future disputes you may face.

Reaching the end of this guide gives you more than knowledge about how to complain. It gives you a clear and practical set of skills that will help you in future interactions with financial firms, service providers, and public bodies. These skills are not limited to banking disputes. They are universal skills that help you protect your rights, express your position clearly, and challenge unfair decisions. This part of the conclusion brings these skills together and shows how you can use them with confidence in the real world.

The first skill you have gained is the ability to recognise when something is not right. Many people accept poor service because they believe they have no choice or because they do not know how to challenge it. Understanding the structure of complaints, the regulatory expectations placed on banks, and the standards required by the Ombudsman allows you to identify when something has gone wrong. You now know the signs of poor handling. You understand when timelines are breached. You can recognise when a response is vague or incomplete. You understand what evidence should have been considered. Recognition is the first step toward action. Without it, unfair outcomes go unchallenged.

The second skill is the ability to structure your concerns. Complaints fail when they are unfocused, overly emotional, or unclear. You learned how to create a clear and precise account of what happened. You learned how to present facts in a timeline. You learned how to explain the impact calmly and effectively. You learned how to describe what you want without making demands. This structure gives you authority. It makes your position strong. It prevents the bank from misunderstanding you or dismissing your complaint due to lack of clarity. Structured communication is one of the most powerful tools in any dispute.

The third skill is the ability to support your argument with evidence. Evidence is the foundation of fairness. You learned how to identify key pieces of evidence, such as call recordings, screenshots, logs, and written communication. You learned how to explain why each piece of evidence matters. You learned how to present evidence in a clear and organised way. This skill protects you from weak or inaccurate responses. It also strengthens your position if you escalate the matter to the Ombudsman. Evidence transforms a complaint from an emotional expression into a well-supported challenge.

The fourth skill is understanding how to challenge a decision effectively. Most people do not know how to challenge a weak complaint response. They may express frustration, but frustration does not influence banks or the Ombudsman. You learned how to challenge using clear headings, factual explanations, and targeted points. You learned to avoid emotion and to stay focused on the facts. This skill requires discipline. It requires calm thinking. It requires structure. Challenging effectively increases the chance that the investigation will be corrected and strengthens the case before the Ombudsman.

Another important skill is understanding how to prepare for escalation. Escalation without preparation weakens your position. You learned how to review the bank's file, identify gaps, organise your evidence, and present your case to the Ombudsman in a simple and factual way. You learned that the Ombudsman responds to clarity, not volume. You learned which details matter most to the Ombudsman. You learned how to avoid common mistakes, such as repeating the entire complaint or relying on emotional descriptions rather than evidence. Preparation is the foundation of a strong escalation.

You also learned how the Ombudsman forms a decision. Understanding this process gives you more confidence. It removes uncertainty. It shows you what matters and what does not. You learned that the Ombudsman reviews evidence independently. You learned that they consider the rules, the timeline, the impact, and your circumstances. You learned that the Ombudsman does not take sides. They follow the fairness test. Understanding how the Ombudsman works helps you prepare stronger submissions and understand the likely outcome.

Another skill you gained is the ability to interpret reasoning. Reasoning is central to any decision. You learned how to assess whether reasoning is complete, logical, and consistent. You learned how to spot incorrect assumptions. You learned how to identify gaps in the analysis. This skill helps you challenge responses from both the bank and the Ombudsman. It also helps you understand decisions more clearly and evaluate whether further action is needed.

The next skill is understanding how to make decisions after the final decision. Many people feel uncertain at this stage. They do not know what rejecting the decision means. They do not know whether litigation is realistic. They do not understand the implications of each route. You learned how to evaluate these choices carefully. You learned when legal action is suitable, when negotiation is possible, and when further action may not be practical. This clarity reduces stress and helps you make informed decisions that protect your interests.

Another important lesson from this guide is the value of calm communication. At every stage of the complaints process, clarity and calmness are more effective than emotion or confrontation. Banks and the Ombudsman respond best to factual, structured communication. You learned how to express clear points without unnecessary language. This style makes it easier for others to understand your position and reduces the risk of your arguments being misunderstood.

Finally, this guide teaches you how to take control of the complaints process. Control is not about being forceful. It is about understanding the rules, knowing your rights, presenting your case clearly, and making informed decisions at each stage. When you understand the process, you reduce uncertainty. You remove the fear that often comes with dealing with large organisations. You protect yourself from unfair outcomes. You ensure that your voice is heard, your evidence is considered, and your position is respected.

This conclusion brings together everything you have learned. It shows that you now have a clear and practical set of tools that make you stronger and more confident when dealing with financial disputes. You understand the process. You understand the rules. You understand how to challenge unfairness. You understand when and how to escalate. You understand how to assess decisions and take further action if needed. These skills remain useful long after this complaint ends. They give you long term protection and confidence in future dealings with financial firms.

Your complaint journey is now complete. You are equipped with the knowledge, structure, and confidence to protect your rights and pursue fairness whenever needed.

Don't miss out!

Visit the website below and you can sign up to receive emails whenever Rebecca Bailey publishes a new book. There's no charge and no obligation.

https://books2read.com/r/B-A-ABZXE-FGCFI

About the Author

Rebecca Bailey writes to make consumer rights simple, clear, and practical. She grew up watching her family struggle with unfair decisions, confusing letters, and poor treatment from large organisations. Those early experiences shaped her belief that fairness only works when people understand their rights. After more than a decade working in complaint resolution across banks, councils, and regulated industries, she saw how often organisations rely on assumptions, poor communication, or incomplete investigations. These patterns taught her where consumers are most vulnerable and how clarity can change outcomes.

Rebecca now writes books that empower readers to challenge unfair decisions with confidence. Her work strips away jargon and focuses on real steps that help people stay in control. She believes that fairness should not depend on how articulate someone is or how well they understand complex systems. Her aim is simple. Give people the knowledge they need to protect themselves and ensure organisations treat them with the respect they deserve.

www.ingramcontent.com/pod-product-compliance
Lightning Source LLC
LaVergne TN
LVHW090420210926
848480LV00002B/631
* 9 7 9 8 2 3 2 6 8 5 6 9 0 *